5 Readings include description, exposition, narration, as well as authentic documents relating to work, school, housing, and shopping.

6 Audio icon indicates that the reading is included in the audio program.

7 Numbering of paragraphs helps teachers and students locate information efficiently.

---

4 Discuss

Find classmates ~~who~~ these steps:

★ Read one statement to a classmate. Ask that person to sign under "agree" or "disagree."

★ Choose another classmate and read another statement. Continue until you have a signature next to each one of the statements.

	AGREE	DISAGREE
EXAMPLE: Everybody should learn English.	*Laura*	_____
1. Everybody should go to school.	_____	_____
2. Women can do the same work as men.	_____	_____
3. The police in this city don't help people.	_____	_____
4. Government workers get too much money.	_____	_____
5. This school should give books to the students.	_____	_____
6. Taxes are too high in this state.	_____	_____
7. Most rich people don't work very hard.	_____	_____
8. Men should help their wives with the housework.	_____	_____
9. Young people should work after school.	_____	_____
10. Pets are helpful in a house.	_____	_____
11. Hospitals and doctors should be free.	_____	_____
12. Every citizen should vote in an election.	_____	_____

---

3 Read

A. Read about choosing leaders in the following passage.

B. Use the glossary on pages 98–103 to learn about new words.

NOTE:
You can find all of the words in blue in the glossary.

Choosing Leaders

1 People make choices every day. They like some things and dislike others. In general, people choose the things they like. Some choices are not very important, but others are very important.

2 People choose to drink coffee or to drink tea. They choose to eat eggs or not to eat them. These choices are important only to the people who make them. They do not change the way we live or the way our government is run.

3 In the United States, citizens can choose the leaders of their cities, of their states, and of the country. Choosing leaders for public office is called voting. Every citizen who is at least 18 years old can vote in local, state, and national elections.

1960 presidential candidates: Richard M. Nixon and John F. Kennedy

4 The way people vote can be very important because elected leaders make laws that can change people's lives. To make good choices, people need to know what each candidate wants to do. This is called the candidate's platform. People need to listen to the candidates, read newspapers, watch the news on television, listen to news on the radio, and talk to other people. Voters discuss the candidates' ideas and decide which candidate they agree with the most.

C. For each of the statements below, circle TRUE or FALSE.

1. People in the United States vote for coffee.	TRUE	(FALSE)
2. U.S. citizens who are 18 or older can vote.	TRUE	FALSE
3. Americans vote for city leaders.	TRUE	FALSE
4. If you want to vote in the U.S., you have to be a citizen.	TRUE	FALSE
5. Voters cannot disagree with the candidates.	TRUE	FALSE

8 Blue type cues students that the word is included in the glossary at the back of the book.

9 Frequent repetition of vocabulary and ideas helps ensure comprehension. Activity types include true-false, fill-in, and multiple-choice activities. Students are also asked to answer questions, identify speakers, identify main ideas and details, and evaluate the information given in a reading.

10 Discuss activities allow students to *apply* information from the first reading in class discussions and to prepare for the second reading.

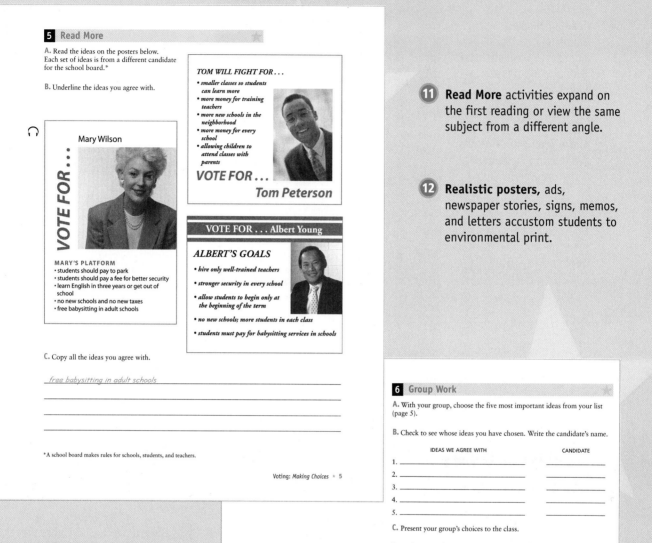

5 Read More

A. Read the ideas on the posters below. Each set of ideas is from a different candidate for the school board.*

B. Underline the ideas you agree with.

Mary Wilson

VOTE FOR . . .

MARY'S PLATFORM
- students should pay to park
- students should pay a fee for better security
- learn English in three years or get out of school
- no new schools and no new taxes
- free babysitting in adult schools

TOM WILL FIGHT FOR . . .
- *smaller classes so students can learn more*
- *more money for training teachers*
- *more new schools in the neighborhood*
- *more money for every school*
- *allowing children to attend classes with parents*

VOTE FOR . . .
Tom Peterson

VOTE FOR . . . Albert Young

ALBERT'S GOALS
- *hire only well-trained teachers*
- *stronger security in every school*
- *allow students to begin only at the beginning of the term*
- *no new schools; more students in each class*
- *students must pay for babysitting services in schools*

C. Copy all the ideas you agree with.

<u>free babysitting in adult schools</u>
_____
_____
_____

*A school board makes rules for schools, students, and teachers.

---

11 **Read More** activities expand on the first reading or view the same subject from a different angle.

12 **Realistic posters,** ads, newspaper stories, signs, memos, and letters accustom students to environmental print.

13 **Group Work** activities allow students to integrate what they have learned. The teacher-student and student-student interaction adds a level of real-time communication that enhances the learning experience.

14 **Vocabulary Review** is a matching or cloze activity that reinforces the topic vocabulary.

---

6 Group Work

A. With your group, choose the five most important ideas from your list (page 5).

B. Check to see whose ideas you have chosen. Write the candidate's name.

IDEAS WE AGREE WITH	CANDIDATE
1. _____	_____
2. _____	_____
3. _____	_____
4. _____	_____
5. _____	_____

C. Present your group's choices to the class.

D. Hold a class election to see which candidate would win.

Vocabulary Review

Match the words on the left with their meanings on the right.

1. <u>B</u> vote   A. person who wants to be elected

2. ____ citizen   B. choose leaders

3. ____ government   C. group of people who make laws for a country or part of a country

4. ____ law   D. person who can vote

5. ____ candidate   E. rule for living

6. ____ election   F. process of choosing a candidate

7. ____ platform   G. what a candidate wants to do

Contents

To the Teacher

Welcome to *Rights and Responsibilities*.

This book has two main purposes. First, as a civics text, it introduces students to concepts that are fundamental to participating in American society. Second, as a reading skills text, *Rights and Responsibilities* also provides multiple opportunities for English language learners to practice and develop new reading and other language skills in a communicative setting.

The organizing principle of *Rights and Responsibilities* is based on the conviction that United States citizens are guaranteed certain political rights. However, it is understood that part of the price of these rights is the concomitant duty to act responsibly. The eight topics chosen for the book are treated in both ways: first as a right, then as a responsibility. Odd number chapters focus on rights, and even number chapters emphasize responsibilities.

The setting for each pair of chapters touches the lives of many immigrants. For example, we know that 85 percent of adult English language students are working and that a large percentage of them have children in school. Therefore, four sets of readings and activities revolve around work and school. Each of the other topics, which include voting, the news media, housing, and health care, is of fundamental importance in the lives of adult immigrant students. The readings and activities arising from these topics are designed to inform learners about their rights and responsibilities as participants in American society while, at the same time, engaging them in language development. As teacher, you are the catalyst for this interaction.

It is likely that some of the ideas contained in this book will be very new for some learners and may even conflict with their cultural norms and world views. In these situations, part of the language teacher's role is to become an interpreter of new ideas and a facilitator of cross-cultural insight.

Each chapter has a set pattern to help the students learn the content of the chapter.

> 1. **Talk About It** introduces a picture and a few questions to stimulate pre-reading discussion. There are no right or wrong answers to the questions. They often call for the students to discuss their lives and ideas. The questions give the teacher the opportunity to

develop concepts and vocabulary that will appear in the two readings to follow. As in the activities that follow, answers to the questions need to be discussed. Simply acknowledging a correct response cuts the discussion short. Look for conversation and debate in the class. Once students feel comfortable with you and their classmates, stimulate a verbal interchange. Questions like "Why do you say that?" or "Do other people have another idea?" can lead to an active, meaningful discussion in which students can try out their communication skills. An open class discussion can also give teachers insight into students' background knowledge of the topic and their linguistic preparation for the activities that follow.

2. **Get Ready to Read** introduces a concept and vocabulary for the first reading. It may be an individual or group activity. The teacher should take the opportunity to discuss the answers with the class and allow for discussion among the students.

3. **Read** can be approached in a number of different ways. Choral reading, silent reading, readers' theater, paragraph reading, and many other techniques can be employed depending on the structure of the texts.

Words that are printed in blue in the readings can be found in the glossary in the back of the book (pages 98–103). Students may be directed to look up these words and treat them as new vocabulary. Classroom "word walls" can be built by writing new vocabulary on slips of paper and posting them in the room. In addition, students can make flash cards or compile personal dictionaries to use for review and practice.

Following each reading, there is a comprehension check to help learners focus on important ideas and details. These activities also allow the teacher to see how well the text was understood. Poor performance on a comprehension check signals that the reading needs to be revisited and individual items on the check further explained or discussed.

4. **Discuss** encourages students to work with the whole class or in small groups to use information from the first reading and prepare for the second.

5. **Read More** expands on the concepts touched upon in the first reading and can be approached in the same manner.

6. **Group Work** provides an opportunity for students to expand on what they have learned by gathering new information and by working with their peers.

7. **Vocabulary Review** is a matching or cloze activity to help students review and consolidate the key vocabulary introduced in the readings.

Appendix A (pages 98–103) provides a glossary with definitions of all of the key vocabulary introduced in the readings. Appendix B (pages 104–108) offers a comprehensive list of the 100 Citizenship Questions applicants may be asked in their oral interviews. Finally, Appendix C (pages 109–112) provides lyrics for a variety of American songs and pledges.

As language teachers, our role is to stimulate communication in English while introducing important concepts that will help improve learners' lives. We believe that this book is a good tool for you to do just that.

To the Student

Welcome to *Rights and Responsibilities*.

Americans believe that they have rights that no government can take away. The Founding Fathers (George Washington, Thomas Jefferson, Benjamin Franklin, and others) believed that all people have political rights.

When you have *rights*, you also have *responsibilities*. Responsibilities are things that you have to do. All members of a society need to think about other people. It is like your family. We all need to think about others.

The chapters in this book work together. One chapter will talk about a *right* of people who are in the United States. The next chapter will talk about a *responsibility* of people who are in the United States.

In this book, you will remember things that you did. You will tell your friends your ideas. You will listen to others. You will talk with others. This will help you develop your English.

In this book, you do not have to say something that you don't believe. But it is important to say something. The classroom is a place to practice your English. It is a place to have fun.

In this book, you will work alone sometimes, and sometimes you will work with classmates. Try to participate. Talk, draw, write, ask questions, answer questions, and read. Nobody will do everything well the first time. You will do the activities many times, so you will get a lot of practice.

Enjoy the book. Try the activities. Develop your English.

Stephen Sloan

CHAPTER 1

LEARNING FOCUS

Content:
* Making and discussing choices
* Voting for choices

Reading:
* Getting general information from a text
* Identifying listed ideas

Language:
* Agreeing and disagreeing
* Making lists

Voting:
Making Choices

1 Talk About It

Discuss these questions with your class.

* What are these people doing?
* Why do people vote?
* Who can vote in the United States?
* Who can vote in another country you know?
* Why do some people choose not to vote?

1

A. Choose the things you like and the things you don't like from each group. Write them on the correct side of the chart. Add one or more things of your own on both sides.

1. eggs, potatoes, fish, chocolate

2. flying in an airplane, riding on a roller coaster, riding on a public bus, driving long distances

3. talking about current events, watching television, reading newspapers, telling people what I like and don't like

Things I Like	**Things I Don't Like**
chocolate	

B. Compare answers with a partner.

EXAMPLE: I like chocolate, riding on a roller coaster, . . .
I don't like eggs, flying in an airplane, . . .

A. Read about choosing leaders in the following passage.

B. Use the glossary on pages 98–103 to learn about new words.

> **NOTE:**
> You can find all of the words in blue in the glossary.

Choosing Leaders

1   People make choices every day. They like some things and dislike others. In general, people choose the things they like. Some choices are not very important, but others are very important.

2   People choose to drink coffee or to drink tea. They choose to eat eggs or not to eat them. These choices are important only to the people who make them. They do not change the way we live or the way our **government** is run.

1960 presidential candidates: Richard M. Nixon and John F. Kennedy

3   In the United States, **citizens** can choose the leaders of their cities, of their states, and of the country. Choosing leaders for public office is called voting. Every citizen who is at least 18 years old can vote in local, state, and national **elections.**

4   The way people vote can be very important because elected leaders make **laws** that can change people's lives. To make good choices, people need to know what each **candidate** wants to do. This is called the candidate's platform. People need to listen to the candidates, read newspapers, watch the news on television, listen to news on the radio, and talk to other people. Voters discuss the candidates' ideas and decide which candidate they agree with the most.

C. For each of the statements below, circle TRUE or FALSE.

1. People in the United States vote for coffee.   TRUE   (FALSE)

2. U.S. citizens who are 18 or older can vote.   TRUE   FALSE

3. Americans vote for city leaders.   TRUE   FALSE

4. If you want to vote in the U.S., you have to be a citizen.   TRUE   FALSE

5. Voters cannot disagree with the candidates.   TRUE   FALSE

Find classmates who agree or disagree with the statements below. Follow these steps:

* Read one statement to a classmate. Ask that person to sign under "agree" or "disagree."

* Choose another classmate and read another statement. Continue until you have a signature next to each one of the statements.

	AGREE	DISAGREE
EXAMPLE: Everybody should learn English.	*Laura*	_____
1. Everybody should go to school.	_____	_____
2. Women can do the same work as men.	_____	_____
3. The police in this city don't help people.	_____	_____
4. Government workers get too much money.	_____	_____
5. This school should give books to the students.	_____	_____
6. Taxes are too high in this state.	_____	_____
7. Most rich people don't work very hard.	_____	_____
8. Men should help their wives with the housework.	_____	_____
9. Young people should work after school.	_____	_____
10. Pets are helpful in a house.	_____	_____
11. Hospitals and doctors should be free.	_____	_____
12. Every citizen should vote in an election.	_____	_____

A. Read the ideas on the posters below. Each set of ideas is from a different candidate for the school board.*

B. Underline the ideas you agree with.

TOM WILL FIGHT FOR . . .

- *smaller classes so students can learn more*
- *more money for training teachers*
- *more new schools in the neighborhood*
- *more money for every school*
- *allowing children to attend classes with parents*

VOTE FOR . . .

Tom Peterson

Mary Wilson

VOTE FOR . . .

MARY'S PLATFORM
- students should pay to park
- students should pay a fee for better security
- learn English in three years or get out of school
- no new schools and no new taxes
- free babysitting in adult schools

VOTE FOR . . . Albert Young

ALBERT'S GOALS

- *hire only well-trained teachers*
- *stronger security in every school*
- *allow students to begin only at the beginning of the term*
- *no new schools; more students in each class*
- *students must pay for babysitting services in schools*

C. Copy all the ideas you agree with.

free babysitting in adult schools _____

_____

_____

_____

*A school board makes rules for schools, students, and teachers.

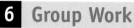

6 Group Work

A. With your group, choose the five most important ideas from your list (page 5).

B. Check to see whose ideas you have chosen. Write the candidate's name.

	IDEAS WE AGREE WITH	CANDIDATE
1.	_____	_____
2.	_____	_____
3.	_____	_____
4.	_____	_____
5.	_____	_____

C. Present your group's choices to the class.

D. Hold a class election to see which candidate would win.

Vocabulary Review ★ ★ ★ ★ ★ ★ ★ ★ ★ ★ ★ ★

Match the words on the left with their meanings on the right.

1. _B_ vote
2. ____ citizen
3. ____ government
4. ____ law
5. ____ candidate
6. ____ election
7. ____ platform

A. person who wants to be elected
B. choose leaders
C. group of people who make laws for a country or part of a country
D. person who can vote
E. rule for living
F. process of choosing a candidate
G. what a candidate wants to do

CHAPTER 2

Content:
- ★ Valuing opinions of others
- ★ Role of the majority and the minority

Reading:
- ★ Following a story line
- ★ Interpreting concepts

Language:
- ★ Approving and disapproving
- ★ Writing and explaining ideas

Voting:
Respecting Choices

1 Talk About It

Discuss these questions with your class.

- ★ What topics do you talk about in your class?
- ★ What topics do you sometimes disagree with family or friends about?
- ★ What topics would you like to discuss more in English?

A. Some students in a class want to have a party, and some students do not. Read the statements below. Decide whether you agree or disagree with each idea. Write *agree* or *disagree* after each statement.

EXAMPLE: "I don't like parties. Parties are a waste of time."   *disagree*

1. "School will be more interesting if we have a party once in a while."   _____

2. "I come to school to study, not to party."   _____

3. "Food is too expensive. We should save money and not have a class party."   _____

4. "We can practice speaking English at the party."   _____

5. "I work hard all day. A party will help me relax."   _____

6. "We shouldn't have a party if my friends can't come."   _____

7. "A party is nice, but who will clean up?"   _____

8. "A party in the middle of the week is a bad idea."   _____

9. "I work hard all day. I want to study at school."   _____

10. "A party will help the students get to know each other and make the class easier for us."   _____

B. Choose two statements you approve of. Write them here.

_____

_____

C. Choose two statements you disapprove of. Write them here.

_____

_____

A. Read about a class election in the story below.

B. Use the glossary on pages 98–103 to learn about new words.

NOTE:
You can find all of the words in blue in the glossary.

The Majority Wins

1   Some of the students in an evening class at the Pine Street Adult School wanted to have a party. They presented their idea to the rest of the class. They wrote all the **reasons** for having a party on a poster.

2   Some of the students didn't want to have a party. They wrote all their reasons for not having a party on a different poster.

3   The teacher and the class discussed the two posters. While one student talked, the others listened. After everybody had a chance to speak, the class had an election.

4   When the votes were counted, the class could see that more than half of the students voted for the party. The majority of the students wanted to have a party. The minority, less than half of the class, voted against the party.

5   A group of more than half the voters is a majority. A group with less than half of the voters is a minority. In an election, the majority wins. The class will have a party.

Should we have a party?

YES	NO
ٰ卌 卌	卌 卌
卌 卌	卌 III
III	
23 votes majority	18 votes minority

C. Fill in each of the sentences below with a word from the story.

1. The students in the class made two _____*posters*_____.

2. In the class _____, the students voted for or against having a party.

3. More than half of any group is called a _____.

4. Less than half of any group is called a _____.

5. In the Pine Street Adult School class, the majority _____ to have a party.

A. Get together with at least four of your classmates. Use one piece of paper. Each person will write one idea about the topic *voting*. Follow these steps:

1. Each person writes down an idea. When one person in the group finishes writing an idea, pass the paper on to the next person.

2. When everyone in the group has finished writing, one person reads all of the ideas aloud.

3. Choose three ideas and talk about them. You can agree or disagree with the idea. Each person should talk at least one time.

4. Choose the best idea in your group.

B. Share your group's best idea with the whole class. Make a poster showing all the groups' ideas about voting.

5 Read More

A. Read more about the roles of the majority and the minority.

B. Use the glossary on pages 98–103 to learn about new words.

Respecting Choices

1   In a **democracy,** all of the adult citizens can vote in elections. By voting, the people make choices about how their government works.

2   In an election, the majority wins and the minority loses. However, the majority cannot forget the minority. The two groups must still live together. Being in the minority means you accept the choice of the majority. Being in the majority means you **respect** the minority.

3   People who are in the minority must **cooperate** with the majority. They can try again to get what they want at the next election. For now, they must go along with what more than 50% of the voters want.

4   Respecting each other will help us to live together better. In the United States, people are free to tell everyone what they think, but they should also respect the opinions of others. Each election gives all sides the chance to say and vote for what they want.

C. Choose the best meaning (A or B) for each idea.

1. The majority wins the election.

    A. The minority is wrong.
    B. The majority gets the most votes.

2. In a democracy, people make choices.

    A. All citizens can vote in an election.
    B. A small group of people decide how the government works.

3. The majority cannot forget the minority.

    A. The losers of an election will never get their ideas heard.
    B. The winners of an election must respect the ideas of all the citizens.

4. The minority must live with the choice of the majority.

    A. The losers of an election must fight to stop the majority's ideas.
    B. The losers of an election should cooperate with the winners and wait for another chance to win.

5. The two groups must still live together.

    A. The minority and the majority have to get along with each other.
    B. The minority has to be silent until the next election.

6 Group Work ★

A. Talk with your group about what the minority and the majority can do to respect each other. Use elections you know about as examples.

EXAMPLE: *In the adult class, the minority can help out at the party.*

B. Make two lists of actions.

1. What can the minority do to show respect for the majority?

2. What can the majority do to show respect for the minority?

MINORITY ACTIONS	MAJORITY ACTIONS
help out at party	

Vocabulary Review

Match the words on the left with their meanings on the right.

1. __C__ democracy   A. 50%

2. _____ respect   B. value

3. _____ neighbors   C. all citizens vote

4. _____ win   D. have a different idea

5. _____ half   E. people who live near you

6. _____ disagree   F. triumph

News Media:
Learning About the World

1 Talk About It ★

Discuss these questions with your class.

★ How do you learn about the events of the world?

★ What is your favorite way of getting the news?

★ What kind of news are you most interested in? Why?

★ Why is it important for people to know what is happening in the world?

A. Discuss the four ways of getting news that are shown in these pictures.

B. In the chart below, list one advantage and one disadvantage of each type of media.

Possible answers: pictures, no pictures, more detail in news stories, hard to use, you can do other things while you learn the news, short reports, links to other information.

	ADVANTAGE	DISADVANTAGE
Television		
Newspapers		
Radio		
Websites		

C. Compare answers with a classmate. Then get together with another pair and discuss all of your answers.

D. Look at the pictures at the top of this page again and discuss these questions with your group.

1. What do you think the TV news story is about?

2. Which groups of people do you think will be most interested in the story?

3 Read

A. Read the newspaper story below. Look for the main event.

B. Use the glossary on pages 98–103 to learn about new words.

NOTE:
You can find all of the words in blue in the glossary.

headline ——— **Mayor Asks For 100 New Officers**

subhead ——— **Will ask City Council for money for cops**

byline ——— By Art Gorlick

dateline ——— Los Arboles – In a speech today, Mayor Rose Collins said she would ask the City Council to vote for enough money to hire more than 100 new police officers. Reacting to the widespread feeling that criminals are taking over the streets of the metropolitan area, the mayor told her audience that there is no more important duty of government than "to protect the people." ——— lead paragraph

Faced with an outcry against more taxes and the economic problems of the state, the mayor said, "We need to make people feel safe, or they will leave the city. Then we will have no economic base upon which to build our future." ——— direct quote

▶ *OFFICERS*, page A12 ——— continuation

C. Write complete answers to each question.

EXAMPLE: Who is the mayor?   *Rose Collins*

1. Is this story local, national, or international news?

_____

2. What did the mayor say she was going to do?

_____

3. What reason did she give for her decision?

_____

D. Look at the story again. Which parts give you the following information? Fill in the right side of the chart.

the name of the story	*headline*
the main event of the story	
the name of the person who wrote the story	
the place where the main event took place	
where to look to continue reading the story	

A. Work with a small group of classmates to plan a radio news show. Follow these guidelines:

★ The radio station you work for has a five-minute news show every hour. It takes about one minute to read each story. There is a one-minute commercial after the second news story.

★ From the list of stories below, choose four to read on the next news show. Then write them in the order they will be read on the air.

News Stories

1. Local house burns down, young girl saved.
2. Dress factory to close, 175 jobs lost.
3. President wants more money to pay for medicine for elders.
4. Soccer fans in Germany fight on playing field.
5. The weather today will be partly sunny with a chance of afternoon showers.
6. Mothers want more stoplights near schools.
7. Two city restaurants closed because of dirty kitchens.
8. Senator Watson, of our state, sent to hospital with a heart problem.
9. Navy finds a boat with narcotics near the coast.
10. Today's sports scores.

Our News Show

_____

_____

Commercial

_____

_____

B. Compare your group's show with those of others in the class.

A. Read more about the news media in the following passage.

B. Use the glossary on pages 98–103 to learn about new words.

🎧 # A Media-Rich World

1   Today, there is almost too much news. It is hard to know what to believe, where to go to get good information, and how to decide what is the best information.

2   Most of us get news of the world from only a few places. Some people hear the news on a radio or watch television to get information about what is happening in the world. Other people read newspapers and magazines or go to Internet Websites. A few people wait to hear what is new in the world from their family or friends.

3   In today's world, people can get information from many different sources. Each source is called a medium. Television is a medium of information; so is radio. Newspapers, books, magazines, telephones, and letters are also forms of media.

4   There are also newer ways of communicating.

5   Today, people use **electronic** media to keep in touch with each other and to find out about the events of the day. Right now most of us are near a cell phone. If we do not have one, somebody near us does. Some cell phones can send pictures as well as voice. They are **visual** ways of communicating. Fax machines can send information as fast as a phone call. Computers are another source of information. E-mail has become a very popular way of communicating, and the Internet has made it possible for news to speed from one part of the world to another in an instant.

6   In a world with so much information, it is difficult to know if all of it is true. We must be careful about what we hear and see. To really understand what is going on, it is a good idea to get the news from more than one place. We must learn to use media in a way that shows us the facts and helps us understand events as they happen.

C. Discuss the following questions with a partner.

1. Which media do you use to learn about daily events?

2. How do you decide if a medium is telling the truth? Name three ways.

3. Where can you go to check media from another country?

A. With a small group of your classmates, make a list of news items that interest you. For example, you may choose soccer scores, today's weather, or a movie you want to see.

B. Look at a local newspaper and find out which section of the paper tells about the things you and your classmates have listed.

News Item	Name of Section	Letter/Page
yesterday's soccer scores	Sports	C1

Vocabulary Review

Match the words on the left with their meanings on the right.

1. _E_ media   A. a radio or television advertisement
2. ____ headline   B. to send and receive information
3. ____ lead paragraph   C. words that attract a reader to a story
4. ____ dateline   D. the place where a news event happens
5. ____ commercial   E. ways of getting information
6. ____ communicate   F. beginning summary of a news story

CHAPTER 4

LEARNING FOCUS

Content:

★ Evaluating news media

★ Recognizing commercial influences on news media

Reading:

★ Understanding main ideas

★ Understanding detailed descriptions

Language:

★ Differentiating fact from opinion

★ Writing a radio commercial

News Media:

Deciding What to Believe

1 Talk About It

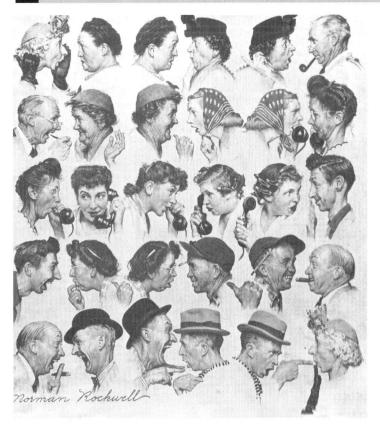

Discuss these questions with your class.

★ What is happening in the picture above?

★ Which news medium do you trust the most: TV, radio, newspapers, or the Internet? Why?

★ How do you decide which information to believe?

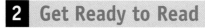

A. A **fact** is a statement that you can prove to be correct. An **opinion** is a statement you believe to be true but cannot prove. Read each sentence and decide if it is a **fact** or an **opinion**. Circle your choice.

1. More than 1,000 people attend this school.   (FACT)   OPINION

2. This school has the best teachers.   FACT   OPINION

3. Seventy-five percent of the students in this school have full-time jobs.   FACT   OPINION

4. Sixteen out of twenty students in this class do not read a newspaper every day.   FACT   OPINION

5. The teachers at this school speak English too fast.   FACT   OPINION

6. More than half the students in this class are female.   FACT   OPINION

7. Women are better cooks than men.   FACT   OPINION

8. Eighty-three percent of the restaurant chefs in this city are men.   FACT   OPINION

9. The average number of stories on a half-hour local news program is fourteen.   FACT   OPINION

10. There is too much violence on TV news shows.   FACT   OPINION

B. Compare your answers with those of your classmates. Give more examples of facts and opinions.

Facts

_____

_____

_____

_____

Opinions

_____

_____

_____

_____

A. Read about facts and opinions in the following passage. Look for the writer's main ideas.

B. Use the glossary on pages 98–103 to learn about new words.

Facts and Opinions in the News

1　News stories should **contain** facts. Reporters from newspapers, television, and radio go out to find information and describe what they see or discover when they talk to people. They try to find out exactly what has happened and report only the facts. They want to tell their readers, viewers, or listeners what actually happened.

2　It is sometimes difficult for reporters to tell only the facts. They may see things that make them sad, happy, or angry. Good reporters do not usually tell or show us how they feel. People **trust** reporters who tell exactly what they see and hear, not what they think or feel about the news.

3　Newspapers often have editorial pages that contain opinions of the newspaper editors as well as those of other writers. Many newspapers also have a place where readers can write letters and tell their opinions about the news.

4　It is important for the news media to keep opinions separate from the facts. If a medium **mixes** opinions and facts in news stories, it is difficult for people to understand what actually happened. As users of media, we must be able to compare the reporting in different media so we can be sure that facts and opinions do not get mixed. In this way, we become smart users of media.

C. For each of the statements below, circle TRUE or FALSE.

1. Reporters try to find the facts in a story.	TRUE	FALSE
2. News stories should mix facts and opinions.	TRUE	FALSE
3. It is easy for reporters to tell only the facts.	TRUE	FALSE
4. You can find opinions about the news on the editorial pages of a newspaper.	TRUE	FALSE
5. Smart users of media only read newspapers.	TRUE	FALSE

A. Read the following description of a news event. Discuss the event with a group of your classmates.

Last night in our city there was a house fire. The night was very cold and the water from the fire hoses froze on the cars and trucks. During the fire, a firefighter carried a child down a ladder from a second-story window. The house is still standing, but the inside was almost completely destroyed.

B. Look at the pictures the photographer brought back from the fire. With a group of classmates, choose the best picture to put next to the newspaper story about the house fire. Be ready to explain why your group chose the photograph.

A. Read more about the media in the newspaper column below.

B. Use the glossary on pages 98–103 to learn about new words

On the Media

Bob Allen

A weekly column devoted to answering your questions about the media

How Do They Make Money?

Dear Bob:
I hear that a TV star can make millions of dollars each year, but I get my television shows for free. All I have to do is turn on the set and watch. Where does the television station get all that money to pay a TV star?

Tom Brody
Wilmington, Delaware

Television is big business. Television stations sell time to advertisers who show commercials. It is commercials that make the money that pays the big salaries to the TV stars. The amount of money that the television stations charge depends on how many people are watching their station at a particular time.

If you wanted to sell dishwashing soap, you would pay a lot of money for advertising time if you knew that a lot of dishwashing soap buyers were watching. The television station will pay a lot of money for a star to attract soap buyers. Then the television station will charge an advertiser a lot of money to show a commercial for one minute or less. If the television station can attract a lot of people to watch, then they can sell a lot of expensive minutes to advertisers. For example, a popular sports show charges more than $100,000 for thirty seconds of advertising time.

Bob Allen

C. Discuss the following questions with a small group of your classmates.

1. If you were an advertiser in a newspaper, what would make you happy?

2. If you were a reporter, what would you think about when you wrote a story?

3. If you chose the news for a news show, how do you think a list of advertisers would help you choose the stories to broadcast?

4. How do you think advertising on television changes the news?

6 | Group Work

A. Work with a small group of your classmates to plan a radio commercial based on the following information.

1. The Trillius Furniture Company has just designed a new set of bedroom furniture. It is very beautiful and they want their customers to buy a lot of sets.

2. They ask your group to write a radio commercial for their beautiful new bedroom furniture.

3. The Trillius Company will only pay for one minute of time for the commercial.

B. Write an advertisement for the new furniture to sell in a store near your school. Be sure to put in all of the important information, and be sure that the commercial you write lasts exactly one minute. If possible, record your commercial and play it for the class.

Vocabulary Review ★ ★ ★ ★ ★ ★ ★ ★ ★ ★

Choose a word from the box to complete the sentences.

interviews	commercials	facts	viewers	~~opinions~~	trust

My friend is a reporter for a television station in our town. She does not give her _____opinions_____

about the news. She reports only the _____ that she sees and hears. Sometimes, she

_____ people who know more about what happened. The television station broadcasts her

stories and those of other reporters to the television _____. People in our town

_____ my friend because she is a good reporter, and they like the show because it does not

have too many _____.

CHAPTER **5**

Housing:
Living as a Renter

1 Talk About It

Discuss these questions with your class.

- ★ Do you live in an apartment? If yes, what problems do you have?
- ★ Where do you go to get help with housing problems?
- ★ What are some important rules for living in an apartment?

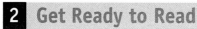

2 **Get Ready to Read**

A. Think about some of the things people want when they rent an apartment. Write your ideas below.

_____ _live in a safe, clean place_ _____

_____

_____

B. Now, make another list of the things apartment _owners_ want when they rent an apartment.

_____ _collect rent every month_ _____

_____

_____

C. Work with a partner to complete the chart below.

	What Renters Want	**What Owners Want**
Things that should always happen	_The electricity should always work._	_People should pay their rent on time._
Things that should frequently happen		
Things that should sometimes happen		
Things that should never happen		

A. Read about living in an apartment in the following passage. Look for the writer's point of view.

B. Use the glossary on pages 98–103 to learn about new words.

A Renter's Story

1   I am living in an apartment for the first time in my life. Before I came here, I lived in a house with my family. I don't live alone. I have **roommates**. We all pay part of the rent to the person who owns the building. She is our **landlord**, and we are her **tenants**.

2   Most of the tenants in our building enjoy apartment life. They can call the landlord when something breaks. They don't have to worry about fixing things themselves.

3   I have neighbors next to my apartment, above my apartment and below my apartment. Sometimes my neighbors are noisy. I call the landlord to **complain** about the noise. The landlord calls my neighbors. When I am too noisy, the landlord calls me.

4   My landlord is worried about the apartment. Sometimes she wants to come in and look around. The landlord owns the apartment, but she cannot come in at any time. She never comes in at night when I am sleeping. I wonder if she comes in during the day when I am at work.

5   My landlord doesn't like parties in the building. She doesn't like a lot of visitors. She worries about noise in the building. She gets upset if the building is not clean. I know she is **concerned** about the people and the building.

6   But she is not my grandmother!

7   The apartment is nice for me for now. Someday I will leave this apartment and get a house for my family and me.

C. Read each statement below and decide who might say it: **tenants** or **landlords** or **both.**

1. _tenants_   "We are noisy sometimes."
2. _____   "I have to pay for repairs to the building."
3. _____   "I don't want the landlord in my apartment."
4. _____   "My sink doesn't work. I want it fixed."
5. _____   "There are too many loud parties at night."

A. Work with at least two classmates. Read each of the sentences below. Put them in order to make a story. Discuss the order as you work. Write the numbers 1 to 8 on the lines next to the sentences to show the correct order.

_____ It was almost midnight before the electrician found the real problem.

_1_ The lights went out in our apartment building after dark last night.

_____ All the renters cheered when the lights went on. Then, they turned them off and went to sleep.

_____ Then, I looked out the window to see if other buildings had electricity and I saw their lights were on.

_____ First, I looked for a flashlight to check the circuit breaker in my apartment and everything was O.K.

_____ The landlord called an electrician to find the problem.

_____ Many tenants called the landlord to report the problem in our building.

_____ He found there was a problem where the electricity entered the building.

B. Write the story here.

_____ _The lights went out_ _____

_____

_____

_____

_____

_____

_____

_____

_____

_____

_____

_____

_____

A. Read more about tenants' rights in the flier below.

B. Use the glossary on pages 98–103 to learn about new words.

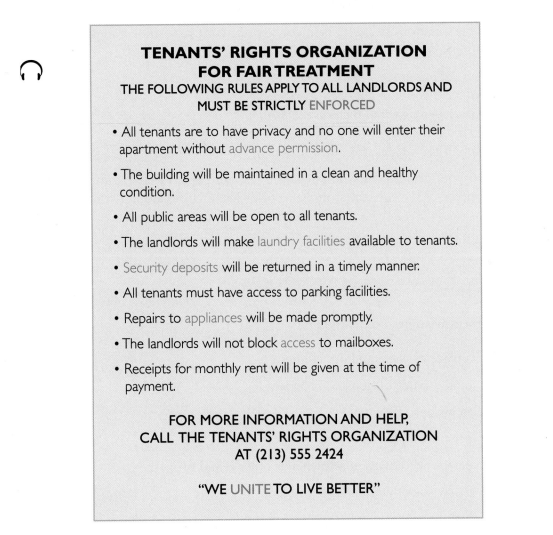

**TENANTS' RIGHTS ORGANIZATION
FOR FAIR TREATMENT**
THE FOLLOWING RULES APPLY TO ALL LANDLORDS AND
MUST BE STRICTLY ENFORCED

- All tenants are to have privacy and no one will enter their apartment without advance permission.
- The building will be maintained in a clean and healthy condition.
- All public areas will be open to all tenants.
- The landlords will make laundry facilities available to tenants.
- Security deposits will be returned in a timely manner.
- All tenants must have access to parking facilities.
- Repairs to appliances will be made promptly.
- The landlords will not block access to mailboxes.
- Receipts for monthly rent will be given at the time of payment.

**FOR MORE INFORMATION AND HELP,
CALL THE TENANTS' RIGHTS ORGANIZATION
AT (213) 555 2424**

"WE UNITE TO LIVE BETTER"

C. According to the tenants' rights flier, what can an apartment owner do? Circle YES or NO.

1. Enter an apartment to check how people are living.	YES	(NO)
2. Keep the building clean.	YES	NO
3. Get permission from tenants to enter their apartments.	YES	NO
4. Keep the security deposit when the tenant leaves.	YES	NO
5. Refuse to fix appliances in an apartment.	YES	NO
6. Let only some renters use the pool.	YES	NO

With a group of your classmates, write a story about a time when a neighbor was noisy. Follow these guidelines:

1. The story does not have to be real. You can make up people, events, and other details to put in the story,

2. Use the questions below to help you get started. Every student in the group has to write at least two sentences.

   When did it happen?
   What were you doing when it happened?
   What was going on in the noisy apartment?
   How did the renters in the building feel about it?
   What did they do to stop the noise?

3. Write your group's story on a separate piece of paper or type it into the computer. Make sure the story has a title. Then read it aloud to the class.

Vocabulary Review ★ ★ ★ ★ ★ ★ ★ ★ ★ ★

Match the words on the left with their meanings on the right.

1. _E_ landlord
2. _____ tenant
3. _____ concerned
4. _____ complain
5. _____ rules
6. _____ enforce
7. _____ appliances
8. _____ laundry facilities
9. _____ security deposit

A. a place to wash and dry clothes

B. money paid to keep an apartment

C. to make someone obey

D. person who lives in an apartment

E. person who owns apartments or other rental property

F. to say something about a problem

G. list of actions a person can or cannot do

H. worried

I. stove, refrigerator, and dishwasher

CHAPTER 6

Housing:
Being a Good Renter

1 | Talk About It

Discuss these questions with your class.

- ★ What are these people doing?
- ★ What are some reasons people move?
- ★ What are some problems people have when they look for a new place to live?
- ★ What do people look for in a place to live?

A. Read each statement and decide if it is something that renters **must** do or something that renters **may** (but do not have to) do. Circle your choice.

1. Pay rent on time.	MAY	MUST
2. Keep apartment clean at all times.	MAY	MUST
3. Keep parties quiet and peaceful.	MAY	MUST
4. Help the landlord keep the building clean.	MAY	MUST
5. Report all criminal activity.	MAY	MUST
6. Give the landlord information about neighbors.	MAY	MUST
7. Give a key to a neighbor.	MAY	MUST
8. Try to buy a house as soon as possible.	MAY	MUST
9. Clean the apartment very well when they move out.	MAY	MUST
10. Obey all the rules of the building.	MAY	MUST
11. Share meals with neighbors.	MAY	MUST
12. Become friends with the landlord.	MAY	MUST

B. Compare answers with a classmate. Discuss your answers.

C. With your partner, make a list of five things a tenant *must* do and five things a tenant *may* do.

3 Read ⭐

A. Scan the following rental agreement for the answers to these questions.

1. How much is the rent? _____*$1600 each month*_____

2. When is the rent due? _____

3. How many people may live in the apartment? _____

4. How much is the security deposit? _____

B. Read the rental agreement again. Use the glossary on pages 98–103 to learn about new words.

Month-to-Month Rental Agreement

This is an agreement drawn this _14th_ day of ___May___ in the year _2004_ by and between Van Nuys Rental Properties, Inc., known as Lessor, and _Pablo Escobar, Maria Cristina Escobar, and their children , Jesus and Xochil,_ known as Lessee.

It is for the payment of _one thousand six hundred ($1600) dollars_ as rent each month. The Lessor grants for hire the living space at: _9229 Haskell Ave, North Hills, California_ described as _Apartment U-2_ for _two_ adults and _two_ minor children. Rent is due and must be paid on the _15th_ day of each month on the following **conditions and terms:**

Occupants: The apartment must be occupied by the named adults and children.

Pets: No pets unless with the written permission of the Lessor.

Ordinances and **Statutes:** The Lessee must obey all laws of the city, county, and state.

Upkeep of Premises: Lessee must maintain the property in good, clean, and healthful condition at all times.

Failure to pay Rent: If the Lessee does not pay monthly rent in a timely fashion, the Lessor may end this agreement upon a written three-day notice. Lessor may reclaim the property. If the Lessee leaves the property without paying rent, the Lessor may take the contents.

Security Deposit: A security deposit of one thousand dollars ($1000) will be held to make sure the apartment is well maintained. The Lessee may not use the security deposit as part of the last month's rent.

Right of Entry: The Lessor may enter the apartment at all reasonable hours to inspect, make repairs, and make changes to the building. The Lessee gives permission to the Lessor to show the apartment to new tenants or buyers.

Signed:

David Forrest
Witness

Brenda Bermudez
Witness

Pablo Escobar   Maria Escobar
Lessee

Robert Simpson
Van Nuys Rental Properties, Inc., Lessor

C. Write complete answers to each of these questions.

1. What must Mr. Escobar do if he wants to have a dog?

   He must get permission from the lessor.

2. When can the landlord enter the apartment?

   _____

3. What may happen if the lessee fails to pay the rent on time?

   _____

4. Would you sign this agreement? Why or why not?

   _____

A. Work with a partner. Ask at least five people outside of your class this question.

"What is the biggest problem people have living in an apartment?"

Write down their answers and bring them to class.

B. Share your answers with the class.

C. Put the class's answers into a chart. See how many of the answers fit into categories. Give each of the categories a name. Then count how many answers are in each category.

CATEGORY 1 Landlord problems	CATEGORY 2 Neighbor problems	CATEGORY 3 _____	CATEGORY 4 _____
don't repair things			

D. Discuss the categories with the most problems. What are the biggest problems for renters in your community?

 **Read More**

A. Read the signs that follow. Each sign is related to a problem that apartment owners may have. For each sign, decide what the problem is. Write the problem under each sign.

Tenants and Guests *Only*

Salespeople bother tenants.

NO Glass at the POOL

_____

Children *Must* be Accompanied *by Parents*

_____

☞ **Check in with the Manager**

_____

Deliveries in the Rear ▮▮▮➡

_____

Close Gate

_____

SLOW
8 miles per hour

_____

Park in Your Own Space

_____

Watch for Children

_____

A. Read the following list of problems. Then, with a small group of class-mates, choose one to work on.

1. Children leave toys all over the place.

2. Tenants play TVs very loudly.

3. Teenagers play ball in the halls.

4. Tenants leave newspapers on the stairs.

5. Tenants' pets are running around the building.

6. Tenants call the manager late at night.

7. _____ (your idea)

B. Discuss ways of solving the problem. Then, make a sign that will tell tenants what to do.

Vocabulary Review ★ ★ ★ ★ ★ ★ ★ ★ ★ ★

Put the words below into the correct category in the chart.

owner   lessee   belongings   tenant   goods   furniture   occupant   appliances
premises   property   apartment   manager   renter   landlord

Places	People who rent	People who own	Things
		owner	

CHAPTER **7**

CHAPTER **7**

Work:
Protection and Pay

LEARNING FOCUS

Content:
- ★ Understanding workers' rights
- ★ Identifying positive and negative aspects of work

Reading:
- ★ Differentiating main ideas from details
- ★ Getting information from a paycheck

Language:
- ★ Giving reasons
- ★ Writing rules

---

1 **Talk About It**

Discuss these questions with your class.

- ★ What are the different jobs in the picture?
- ★ What is your job? How did you get it?
- ★ What do you have to do to get a better job?
- ★ What jobs do you want for your children?

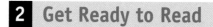

2 **Get Ready to Read**

A. In small groups, write the answers to these questions in the correct circle.

1. What do you like about the work you do?

2. What don't you like about the work you do?

We like . . .

coffee breaks

We don't like . . .

low pay

B. Discuss the reasons for the items in both circles with your group.

EXAMPLE: "I like coffee breaks because I can talk with my friends."

C. Share your group's answers with the whole class. Which answers were mentioned by all or most of the groups? Write them below and discuss each one.

POSITIVES (WE LIKE . . .)　　　　NEGATIVES (WE DON'T LIKE . . .)

_____　　　_____

_____　　　_____

A. Read about workers' rights in the flier below. Look for the important ideas.

B. Use the glossary on pages 98–103 to learn about new words.

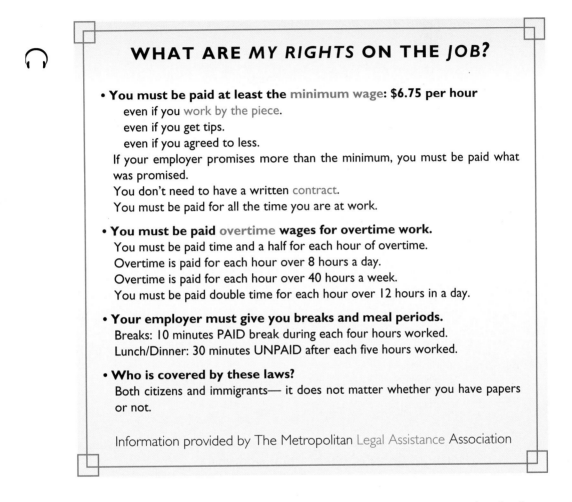

WHAT ARE *MY RIGHTS* ON THE *JOB*?

• **You must be paid at least the minimum wage: $6.75 per hour**
   even if you work by the piece.
   even if you get tips.
   even if you agreed to less.
   If your employer promises more than the minimum, you must be paid what was promised.
   You don't need to have a written contract.
   You must be paid for all the time you are at work.

• **You must be paid overtime wages for overtime work.**
   You must be paid time and a half for each hour of overtime.
   Overtime is paid for each hour over 8 hours a day.
   Overtime is paid for each hour over 40 hours a week.
   You must be paid double time for each hour over 12 hours in a day.

• **Your employer must give you breaks and meal periods.**
   Breaks: 10 minutes PAID break during each four hours worked.
   Lunch/Dinner: 30 minutes UNPAID after each five hours worked.

• **Who is covered by these laws?**
   Both citizens and immigrants— it does not matter whether you have papers or not.

Information provided by The Metropolitan Legal Assistance Association

C. Write two important ideas from the flier on lines 1 and 2. Then write two details about each idea.

1. Important idea: _____

   Detail: _____

   Detail: _____

2. Important idea: _____

   Detail: _____

   Detail: _____

A. Read Mario's story below.

Mario started a new job. He works 40 hours a week and earns $10.00 an hour. He gets paid for two weeks every other Friday.

For the first two weeks, Mario even worked 5 hours overtime.

He got his paycheck today and was very sad. He thought that he would get at least $800 dollars. He did not. The check was only for $646.40.

B. Discuss these questions with a small group of your classmates.

1. Why didn't Mario get the money he expected?

2. What should Mario do?

C. Work with your group. Make a list of some of the reasons that money might be deducted (taken from) a paycheck.

<u>   *United States income tax*   </u>

D. Share your list with the whole class.

5 Read More

A. Read the paycheck below. Notice the important details.

B. Use the glossary on pages 98–103 to learn about new words.

EMPLOYEE NAME				ISSUE DATE
Mario Obero				**6/18/05**

DELAWARE CONSTRUCTION COMPANY
134 W. ADAMS ST., ALLENTOWN, PA 18103

Employee Statement of Earnings

Time	Rate	Gross
80.00	10.00	800.00
5.00	15.00	75.00

TAXABLE GROSS	$875.00
PAYROLL DEDUCTIONS	
FED INCOME TAX	78.75
STATE INCOME TAX	8.75
SOCIAL SECURITY	52.50
STATE UNEMPLOYMENT INSURANCE	8.75
UNION DUES	25.00
HEALTH INSURANCE	45.00
MEDICARE	9.85
NET PAY	$646.40

DELAWARE CONSTRUCTION CO.   0000
134 W. ADAMS ST.
ALLENTOWN, PA 18103

Date **June 18, 2005**

$646.40

Pay to
the order of   **Mario Obero**

Six hundred forty six dollars and forty cents

W. M. Collins
W. M. Collins Treasurer

Allentown Bank of Commerce
:'000000000':   000000000"   0000

C. Use information from Mario's paycheck to answer the questions.

1. Where does Mario work? _Delaware Construction Company_

2. How much money did he make for his work for the two weeks? $_____

3. How many hours did he work overtime? _____ hours

4. How much money did he take home? $_____

5. How much money was withheld for taxes? $_____

6. How much did Mario pay for health insurance? $ _____

7. What percent of Mario's total salary was withheld? _____%

Work: *Protection and Pay* ★ 41

With a group of your classmates, create a list of ten rights that every worker should have.

EXAMPLE: *Every worker should have at least one day of vacation for every month worked.*

1. _____

2. _____

3. _____

4. _____

5. _____

6. _____

7. _____

8. _____

9. _____

10. _____

Vocabulary Review

Match the words on the left with their meanings on the right.

1. __F__ employee

2. _____ employer

3. _____ minimum wage

4. _____ overtime

5. _____ deduction

6. _____ pay stub

7. _____ unemployment insurance

8. _____ take home pay

A. smallest hourly wage a worker can legally get

B. paper that shows how much a worker gets paid and how much is withheld from wages

C. person or company that hires people to work

D. amount of money you keep after deductions

E. hours of work after regular time

F. person who works for a company or someone else

G. a plan to protect workers who lose their jobs

H. money taken out of a paycheck

CHAPTER 8

LEARNING FOCUS

Content:
* ★ Evaluating work rules
* ★ Understanding health benefits

Reading:
* ★ Identifying main ideas and details
* ★ Reading posted rules and memos

Language:
* ★ Giving reasons
* ★ Writing a memo to end a problem

Work:
Getting Along

1 Talk About It

Discuss these questions with your class.

* ★ What is happening in the pictures?
* ★ What are your working hours? What time do you start and finish each day?
* ★ What are some of the things your employer expects of you on the job?
* ★ What do you do to get along with your co-workers?

A. Pretend you are an employer. Read each statement from one of your workers and decide if it is a good reason for not going to work. Circle **good** or **not good.**

1. "I have to help a friend today."   GOOD   NOT GOOD

2. "My child is very sick."   GOOD   NOT GOOD

3. "I am sick with a bad cold."   GOOD   NOT GOOD

4. "We need to visit a friend in the hospital."   GOOD   NOT GOOD

5. "I need to take my husband to the dentist."   GOOD   NOT GOOD

6. "I have to attend a conference with my child's teacher."   GOOD   NOT GOOD

7. "I need to take my car to the mechanic."   GOOD   NOT GOOD

8. "Today is my birthday."   GOOD   NOT GOOD

9. "We are planning a wedding for my son."   GOOD   NOT GOOD

10. "I have a personal problem."   GOOD   NOT GOOD

11. "I'm too tired to go to work today."   GOOD   NOT GOOD

12. "I have to study for a test."   GOOD   NOT GOOD

B. Work with a partner. Choose three statements that are very poor reasons for not going to work. Tell the class what the boss should do when the employee phones in. Follow the example below.

Employee: I have to help a friend today.

Employer: We need your help here. Help your friend after work.

Employee: _____

Employer: _____

Employee: _____

Employer: _____

Employee: _____

Employer: _____

Employee: _____

Employer: _____

A. Read the rules for workers below. Think about which rules are reasonable and which rules are not.

B. Use the glossary on pages 98–103 to learn about new words.

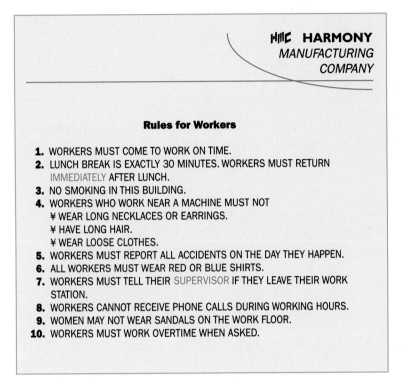

HARMONY *MANUFACTURING COMPANY*

Rules for Workers

1. WORKERS MUST COME TO WORK ON TIME.
2. LUNCH BREAK IS EXACTLY 30 MINUTES. WORKERS MUST RETURN IMMEDIATELY AFTER LUNCH.
3. NO SMOKING IN THIS BUILDING.
4. WORKERS WHO WORK NEAR A MACHINE MUST NOT
   ¥ WEAR LONG NECKLACES OR EARRINGS.
   ¥ HAVE LONG HAIR.
   ¥ WEAR LOOSE CLOTHES.
5. WORKERS MUST REPORT ALL ACCIDENTS ON THE DAY THEY HAPPEN.
6. ALL WORKERS MUST WEAR RED OR BLUE SHIRTS.
7. WORKERS MUST TELL THEIR SUPERVISOR IF THEY LEAVE THEIR WORK STATION.
8. WORKERS CANNOT RECEIVE PHONE CALLS DURING WORKING HOURS.
9. WOMEN MAY NOT WEAR SANDALS ON THE WORK FLOOR.
10. WORKERS MUST WORK OVERTIME WHEN ASKED.

C. Write two rules from the poster that are reasonable and two rules that are unreasonable. Explain why the unreasonable rules are not reasonable.

Reasonable Rules

1. _____

2. _____

Unreasonable Rules

1. _____

Why: _____

_____

2. _____

Why: _____

_____

D. With your classmates, discuss the rules that you think are unreasonable. Do you all agree about the unreasonable rules? How many disagree? Why?

A. Get together with at least three classmates. If you were the management at a manufacturing company, what rules would you make for workers? Write four rules that at least three of you think are reasonable.

_____

_____

_____

_____

B. Share your group's list of rules with the class. Do your classmates think your rules are reasonable or unreasonable?

C. Write five rules that the class thinks are the best.

_____

_____

_____

_____

_____

A. Read the following memo about health benefits. Look for the main ideas and the details.

B. Use the glossary on pages 98–103 to learn about new words.

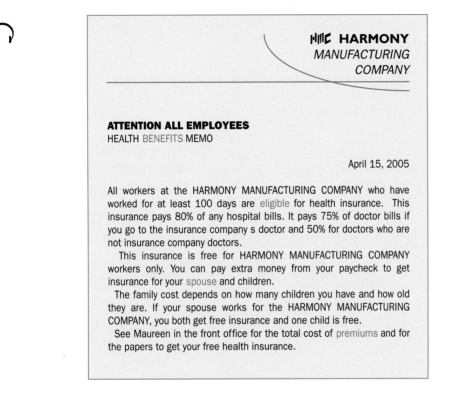

ᕼᕮ HARMONY
MANUFACTURING
COMPANY

ATTENTION ALL EMPLOYEES
HEALTH BENEFITS MEMO

April 15, 2005

All workers at the HARMONY MANUFACTURING COMPANY who have worked for at least 100 days are eligible for health insurance. This insurance pays 80% of any hospital bills. It pays 75% of doctor bills if you go to the insurance company s doctor and 50% for doctors who are not insurance company doctors.

This insurance is free for HARMONY MANUFACTURING COMPANY workers only. You can pay extra money from your paycheck to get insurance for your spouse and children.

The family cost depends on how many children you have and how old they are. If your spouse works for the HARMONY MANUFACTURING COMPANY, you both get free insurance and one child is free.

See Maureen in the front office for the total cost of premiums and for the papers to get your free health insurance.

C. Write complete answers to these questions.

EXAMPLE: What company is this memo from?   *Harmony Manufacturing Company.*

1. What is this memo about?

_____

2. How much money will the insurance company pay if the worker has a hospital bill of $900.00?

_____

3. What does a worker have to do if she wants insurance for her children?

_____

4. What should employees do if they are interested in getting health insurance?

_____

5. What two questions does a worker have to ask before deciding to buy insurance for a family of four (spouse and two children)?

_____

_____

A. Imagine that you and three of your classmates are supervisors at a factory. Many of the workers are leaving work before the end of the work day. Discuss ways of solving the problem.

B. Look at the questions in the graph below. Write a memo to the workers. The memo should end the problem. Include answers to all three questions in your memo.

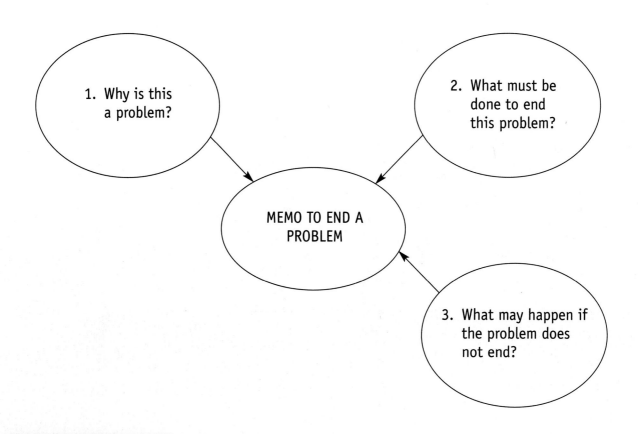

1. Why is this a problem?

2. What must be done to end this problem?

MEMO TO END A PROBLEM

3. What may happen if the problem does not end?

Vocabulary Review ★ ★ ★ ★ ★ ★ ★ ★ ★ ★ ★

Match the words on the left with their meanings on the right.

1. __C__ supervisor   A. payment to an insurance company

2. _____ immediately   B. health insurance, retirement, vacations, etc.

3. _____ spouse   C. person in charge; boss

4. _____ benefits   D. able to get something

5. _____ premium   E. right away; without delay

6. _____ eligible   F. the person you are married to

Right

LEARNING FOCUS

Content:
- ★ Understanding the public school system
- ★ Relating educational level to income

Reading:
- ★ Getting information from a graph
- ★ Scanning for specific information

Language:
- ★ Expressing plans and hopes
- ★ Making generalizations

School:
Education is Power

Discuss these questions with your class.

- ★ What's happening in this picture?
- ★ What are graduations like in a country you know?
- ★ Why do adults go to school?
- ★ What does graduation show about a person?

A. Work with a small group. Look at the graph below and answer this question.

What does this graph tell us about education in the U.S.?

_____

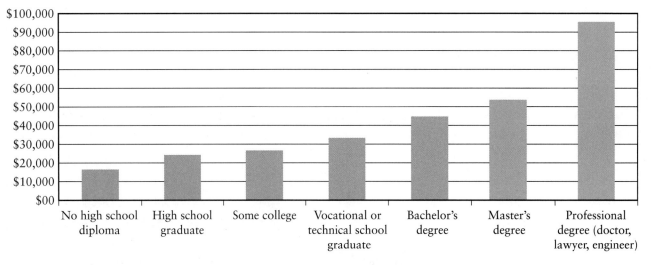

Annual Income by Level of Education in the U.S.

Source: Statistical Abstract of the United States, 2000

B. Share your group's answer with the whole class.

C. Write complete answers to each of the following questions.

EXAMPLE: About how much money can a high school graduate expect to make each year in the United States?

About $24,000 a year.

1. Which group has the highest annual income?

_____

2. What level of education do you plan to reach?

_____

3. What level of education do you hope your children will reach?

_____

A. Read about the American school system in the following passage.

B. Use the glossary on pages 98–103 to learn about new words.

The American School System

1   The United States does not have a single national educational system. Each state has its own **system** for the education of children. In every state there are three **levels** of education.

2   Until children are six years old, they do not have to go to school. Young children may begin kindergarten at the age of five, but six-year-old boys and girls must go to school. In most states, compulsory education ends when students are around seventeen years old.

3   Each state has free public education for all students. Children go to elementary schools for five or six years. Older boys and girls go to free secondary schools, starting at grades six or seven and finishing at grade twelve. Secondary school is compulsory. In some states, children go to a **separate** junior high school for grades seven, eight, and nine. In other states, children go to a separate middle school for grades six, seven, and eight. After that, the students go to high school. When students finish high school successfully, they receive a high school diploma.

4   Secondary schools prepare students to go to a college or university, to start a job, or to begin training for work. In most states, people eighteen years and older can go to adult school to study for a diploma. It is the same as a high school diploma. Adult school is not compulsory, but it is usually free.

5   In the United States, more than half of all children will graduate from high school and get diplomas. More than half of all high school graduates will go to universities or colleges, or they will get more special training. After high school, education is not compulsory, nor is it free.

C. Write the ages of most of the students at each level in the chart below.

Level	Grades	Ages
Elementary	Kindergarten	5
	Grades 1–6	
Middle or Junior High School	Grades 6–8	
	Grades 7–9	
High School	Grades 9–12	
	Grades 10–12	

A. Discuss these questions with a small group of your classmates.

1. How old are your children or younger brothers and sisters or cousins?

2. What profession do you want them to have?

3. How much money can they earn in this profession?

4. Use the information in this chapter to list the types of schools they will have to attend.

B. Talk to the other groups in your class. Discuss the different choices for people after they graduate from high school. Why would someone choose to go to a vocational or technical school instead of college? Do you think going to school after high school is worth the time and expense?

C. Ask one classmate to count the answers to these questions. Copy the totals into the chart.

1. How many parents in the class think their children will go to a college or university?

2. How many parents want their children to go to work after high school?

3. How many parents want their children to go into the armed forces (army, navy, air force)?

COLLEGE OR UNIVERSITY	WORK	ARMED FORCES

D. Discuss the advantages and disadvantages of each of the choices in the chart.

EXAMPLE: College gives my daughter more education, but it is too expensive.

A. Scan the information in the chart in Exercise B for the following details.

1. Number of years to finish an associate's degree: _____

2. Place to get a master's degree: _____ or _____

3. Number of years in law school to become a lawyer: _____

B. Read the chart for general information about degrees in the United States. Use the glossary on pages 98–103 to learn about new words.

Degrees in the United States

DEGREE	SCHOOL	YEARS
diploma	high school	3 or 4
associate of arts or sciences (A.A., A.S.)	community college	2
bachelor of arts or sciences (B.A., B.S.)	college or university	4 or 2 years community college + 2
master of arts or sciences (M.A., M.S.)	college or university	bachelor's + 2
doctor of philosophy (Ph.D.)	university	master's + 2 or more

Doctors, lawyers, and some other professions have more years of studies in professional schools:

DOCTOR: 4 years bachelor's degree + 4 years medical school + 2 years intern + 2 years residency

LAWYER: 4 years bachelor's degree + 3 years law school

TEACHER: 4 years bachelor's degree + 2 years education school

DENTIST: 4 years bachelor's degree + 2 years dental school

All degrees may take longer depending upon how many classes a student can take each year. Bachelor's degrees usually take four years of full-time study to finish.

C. Fill in the missing information in each statement.

1. Most bachelor's degrees take _____ years to finish.

2. A master's degree usually takes _____ years more than a bachelor's degree.

3. Put these degrees in the order in which they are earned.
   _____ Ph.D.   _____ bachelor's   _____ master's

4. To be a doctor of medicine you have to study _____ years after high school.

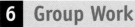

6 Group Work

There are many questions about going to college. With a group of your classmates, write several questions about getting into college, studying at a college, and living at a college. See if any of your classmates can answer the questions or know how to find out the answers. Your teacher can help you.

Questions About College

1. _Where can we get information about how to apply?_ _____

2. _____

3. _____

Vocabulary Review

Match the words on the left with their meanings on the right.

1. __C__ secondary school   A. belonging to the whole country

2. _____ elementary school   B. certificate for finishing high school

3. _____ compulsory   C. school for older children

4. _____ diploma   D. school for younger children

5. _____ community college   E. certificate for finishing college

6. _____ separate   F. something you must do

7. _____ degree   G. not together

8. _____ national   H. place to get an associate's degree

CHAPTER **10**

School:
Helping Your Children

CHAPTER **10**

LEARNING FOCUS

LEARNING FOCUS

Content:

★ Getting involved with children's education

Reading:

★ Categorize information from a list
★ Read an official school letter

Language:

★ Asking for information
★ Writing absence notes

1 Talk About It

Discuss these questions with your class.

★ Who helps children with their homework in your house?

★ When is a good time to do homework?

★ What are some ways a household member can help even if he or she does not understand the homework?

A. Work with a small group. Look at the list below. Decide whether items 1 to 12 are something parents **can** or **cannot** control. Circle your choice.

1. When homework time starts	CAN CONTROL	CANNOT CONTROL
2. Amount of time the TV is on	CAN CONTROL	CANNOT CONTROL
3. How much homework a student has	CAN CONTROL	CANNOT CONTROL
4. Well trained teachers	CAN CONTROL	CANNOT CONTROL
5. Student has a place to study.	CAN CONTROL	CANNOT CONTROL
6. Brothers or sisters help the student.	CAN CONTROL	CANNOT CONTROL
7. Be positive with the student.	CAN CONTROL	CANNOT CONTROL
8. Student reads at home every day.	CAN CONTROL	CANNOT CONTROL
9. Student has social activities.	CAN CONTROL	CANNOT CONTROL
10. Student has good textbooks at school.	CAN CONTROL	CANNOT CONTROL
11. Food in the cafeteria is good.	CAN CONTROL	CANNOT CONTROL
12. Student has nice friends.	CAN CONTROL	CANNOT CONTROL

13. _____

14. _____

B. With your group, think of at least two more things parents can control. Add these as 13 and 14 in the list. Discuss how parents can do all the things they can control.

A. Read about the ways teachers think parents can help children at school.

B. Use the glossary on pages 98–103 to learn about new words.

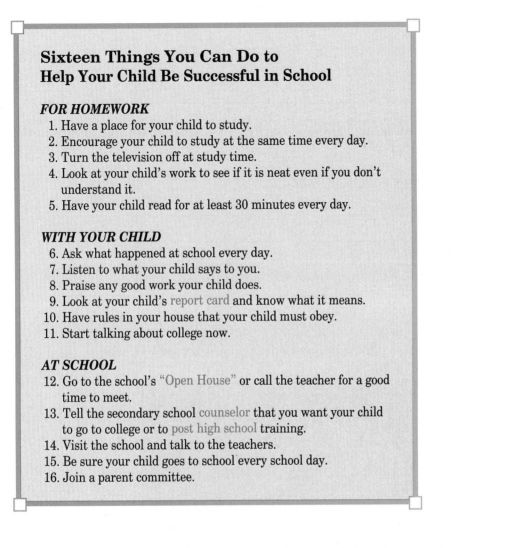

Sixteen Things You Can Do to Help Your Child Be Successful in School

FOR HOMEWORK
1. Have a place for your child to study.
2. Encourage your child to study at the same time every day.
3. Turn the television off at study time.
4. Look at your child's work to see if it is neat even if you don't understand it.
5. Have your child read for at least 30 minutes every day.

WITH YOUR CHILD
6. Ask what happened at school every day.
7. Listen to what your child says to you.
8. Praise any good work your child does.
9. Look at your child's report card and know what it means.
10. Have rules in your house that your child must obey.
11. Start talking about college now.

AT SCHOOL
12. Go to the school's "Open House" or call the teacher for a good time to meet.
13. Tell the secondary school counselor that you want your child to go to college or to post high school training.
14. Visit the school and talk to the teachers.
15. Be sure your child goes to school every school day.
16. Join a parent committee.

C. Write the number of each of the sixteen things in one of the columns in the chart. With a partner, discuss the things you don't know how to do.

1. Things I do now	2. Things I plan to do	3. Things I don't know how to do

4 Discuss

A. Work with a small group. Make a list of questions that parents can ask teachers.

1. _How is my daughter doing in math?_ _____

2. _____

3. _____

4. _____

5. _____

B. Now, make a list of answers that a teacher might give to each of the questions in A.

1. _She's doing all right in class, but she hasn't done all of the_ _homework._ _____

2. _____

3. _____

4. _____

5. _____

C. Share your list of questions and answers with the whole class.

A. Read the letter to parents from the superintendent about absences from school. Look for the acceptable reasons for a child's absence.

B. Use the glossary on pages 98–103 to learn about new words.

🎧

BERNARD UNIFIED SCHOOL DISTRICT
OFFICE OF THE SUPERINTENDENT OF SCHOOLS

Dear Parents or Guardians of Bernard School District Students:

State laws require that students between the ages of 6 years and 17 years attend school every day. Under these laws the student can stay home only under certain circumstances.

A student may stay home if
- the student is ill.
- the student has a medical appointment. (Please schedule regular appointments for after school hours, weekends, or vacation time.)
- there is a death in the student's immediate family.
- the student has a court date.
- it is a religious holiday of your faith.

The school district does not recognize any other excuse for absences.

If a student must miss a day of school, the parent is responsible for writing an absence note. The absence note must contain the date on which the note is written, the name of the student, the date or dates of the absence, the reason for the absence, and the parent or guardian's signature.

If you have any questions about this policy, please contact the principal of your school.

Yours truly,

Jean Bronson

Jean Bronson
Superintendent

Read the absence note that follows and answer the questions.

> APRIL 24, 2004
>
> DEAR MRS. AMES,
>
> JANE JONES WAS ABSENT ON TUESDAY AND WEDNESDAY, APRIL 22 AND 23, BECAUSE SHE HAD TO BABY-SIT HER LITTLE BROTHER.
>
> THANK YOU,
>
> Sally Jones

1. When was the note written? *April 24, 2004* _____

2. Who gets the note? _____

3. How many days was Jane absent? _____

4. Why was she absent? _____

5. Who signed the note? _____

6. Was this an acceptable reason to be absent?   YES   NO

6 Group Work

A. Work with a small group of your classmates. Discuss which of the following reasons for a student to be absent from school are acceptable.

birthday	pay bills	family problems	death in the family
fever	visit an uncle	religious holiday	doctor's appointment
work	go to court	take care of baby	take mother to hospital

B. Choose an acceptable reason and write an absence note for a student. Be sure to put all the required information in your note.

Vocabulary Review ★ ★ ★ ★ ★ ★ ★ ★ ★ ★

Match the words on the left with their meanings on the right.

1. _B_ report card   A. meeting with a teacher about a student

2. ____ open house   B. tells how well a student is doing at school

3. ____ absence note   C. person who gives advice to students

4. ____ conference   D. manager of the school

5. ____ homework   E. time to visit students' classrooms

6. ____ principal   F. tells why a student was not in school

7. ____ policy   G. a set of rules

8. ____ counselor   H. study tasks for outside the classroom

CHAPTER 11

Content:

★ Identifying medical problems

★ Accessing medical care

Reading:

★ Reading for general information and specific details

Language:

★ Categorizing information

★ Describing habitual actions

Health Care:
Finding the Right Medical Care

1 Talk About It

Discuss these questions with your class.

★ What are these people doing?

★ What happens in your house when somebody is ill?

★ Where do you get medical advice?

★ When should people go to a clinic like the one in the picture above?

A. Work with partner. Look at the medical problems in the box below. Look up the words you are not sure about in a good dictionary.

cold	measles	heart attack	runny nose	diabetes
scraped knee	flu	high fever	broken arm	leukemia
cancer	arthritis	stomachache	cough	pneumonia
stroke	diarrhea	rash	indigestion	cut finger

B. Divide the medical problems into two groups: (1) those we can take care of at home and (2) those for which we need to get help from a doctor or hospital.

At Home

cold
_____
_____
_____
_____
_____
_____
_____
_____

Doctor

_____
_____
_____
_____
_____
_____
_____
_____

C. Compare answers with another set of partners. Did you make the same decisions? Discuss the differences, and explain the reasons why you made your choices.

EXAMPLE: "I usually take care of a cough at home, but if it hurts a lot I go to a doctor."

3 Read

A. Read about the American health care system in the following passage.

B. Use the glossary on pages 98–103 to learn about new words.

Finding Health Care

1   The United States does not have a national health care system. Health care is different in every state and in every city. There are many ways people can get help if they are sick.

2   People can go to a **private doctor.** A family doctor will help sick people in the office or **recommend** another **physician** if they need **specialized** medical care. If a person is very sick, a doctor will arrange for him or her to go to a hospital. Private doctors and special doctors charge money for their help.

3   Some doctors work together in clinics to care for their patients. Some clinics are small; others are very big. Some clinics are in hospitals; others are in communities. Because the doctors work together, they can charge less money for their **services.**

4   People who cannot pay for doctors go to **government clinics.** Often these clinics are in big government hospitals. The doctors in the government clinics will help all sick people, but the patients usually have to wait a long time to see a doctor. Government clinics usually charge a lot less money than private clinics. The amount of money people have to pay depends on how much money they earn and the size of their family. Government clinics are supported by **taxes** paid by everyone.

5   Victims who have accidents or serious, sudden **illnesses** go to a hospital emergency room. Doctors and nurses will give them immediate help, then decide what kind of care they will need next. After the emergency, the hospital will send the bill to the patient's home or to the insurance company for payment.

C. Write short answers to the questions below.

1. Write three places where a person can get medical help.

    __*private doctor*__ , _____ , and _____

2. Where would an ambulance take a person who was hurt in a house fire?

    _____

3. Who pays for government clinics?

    _____

4. What is the name of a doctor or clinic in your neighborhood?

    _____

A. Discuss these questions with at least three of your classmates.

1. Whom do you talk to about medical problems?

2. Where do you go to get medical help?

3. What would you say about medical care in your community to people who have just arrived?

4. What do you think about the health care you can get?

5. What are some reasons why people don't go to clinics or doctors?

B. Join another group of four. In the new group, choose two of the questions and discuss them.

C. Select the three most interesting things you have heard in your conversations and write them on the lines below.

_____

_____

_____

D. As a class, make a list of the most interesting information from your discussions on health care.

A. Read about ways of paying for medical services in the following passage.

B. Use the glossary on pages 98–103 to learn about new words.

Paying for Medical Services

1   Medical services are very expensive in the United States. Some people are afraid to go to a doctor because the cost is so high. One visit to a doctor can cost more than $200.

2   Most people cannot afford to pay medical bills by themselves. Health insurance plans will pay all or part of a doctor's bill. To get insurance, a person has to pay a monthly premium to an insurance company. Then, when a large medical bill arrives, the insurance company will pay all or most of it. Under some plans, patients must make a small co-payment each time they visit a doctor or clinic. Most doctors bill the insurance company directly, but others require that the patient pay first. Then the patient has to ask the insurance company for a reimbursement.

3   There are many ways to get insurance. Many people get health insurance as a benefit from their employers. Unions often sell family insurance at low prices. Schools often have special insurance for their students. Some insurance is only for accidents. Some insurance is for any illness.

4   Many big insurance companies sell health insurance to anybody who wants to pay. The insurance company will give a list of doctors and clinics that accept the insurance. For the most savings, a person has to go to doctors and clinics on the list. Health maintenance organizations, or HMOs, are the least expensive type of medical insurance. HMO members save money by using the clinics and services that are provided by the organization.

C. Write complete answers to the questions below.

EXAMPLE: Why are some people afraid to go to a doctor?

The cost of medical services is very high.

1. Why is it important to have health insurance in the United States?

_____

2. Where can people get health insurance if it is not offered at work?

_____

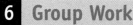

A. Many families have special things they do to make people feel better. Some are old ideas that have been in the family for years. Here are some common problems. Write down what your family does when a family member has these problems. Then think of two more and add them to the list.

PROBLEM	FAMILY REMEDY
sore throat	*drink tea with honey*
cold	_____
cough	_____
hiccoughs	_____
sneezing	_____
stiff neck	_____
sore back	_____
_____	_____
_____	_____

B. Share your list of family remedies with a small group of your classmates. Then choose the most interesting ones to share with the whole class.

Vocabulary Review

Match the words on the left with their meanings on the right.

1. _E_ co-payment
2. ____ clinic
3. ____ emergency room
4. ____ Health Maintenance Organization
5. ____ physician
6. ____ reimbursement
7. ____ illness

A. doctor

B. group of doctors working together

C. place to go for immediate care

D. sickness or disease

E. money paid in addition to insurance

F. money paid back by the insurance company to the patient

G. least expensive kind of insurance

CHAPTER 12

LEARNING FOCUS

Content:
- ★ Choosing healthy food
- ★ Home health care

Reading:
- ★ Interpreting informal advice
- ★ Understanding and following instructions

Language:
- ★ Categorizing information
- ★ Listing suggestions

Health Care:
Preventing Health Problems

1 **Talk About It**

Discuss these questions with your class.

★ What are your favorite foods?

★ Is your lunch (or breakfast) more like the food on the right or the food on the left?

★ What makes food taste good?

A. Work with a partner. Look at the list of foods and drinks. Add five more that you eat or drink.

meatball	hamburger	burrito	egg	pork
beef	fish	chicken	turkey	bacon
tomato	pepper	celery	beans	spinach
lettuce	corn	potato	onion	chili
banana	orange	melon	cantaloupe	lemon
pineapple	bread	sweet roll	doughnut	roll
tortilla	pita	pancake	rice	toast
milk	tea	coffee	soft drink	chocolate milk
pie	cake	ice cream	cream	sugar
salt	butter	margarine	cheese	sour cream
_____	_____	_____	_____	_____

B. Divide the foods in the list in A into the following categories. You can use some foods in more than one category.

foods that are bad for you	*doughnut*
foods that are good for you	
foods that have vitamins	
foods that can make you sick	*sugar*
foods that can make you healthy	*cantaloupe*
foods that are good for you but taste bad	

A. Read advice about healthy eating in the following passage.

B. Use the glossary on pages 98–103 to learn about new words.

Are You What You Eat?

1   There is an old saying, "You are what you eat." If that is true, am I a cow after I eat a hamburger or a corncob after eating a tortilla? Will I be a fish after I eat a tuna sandwich?

2   Obviously, people do not change into the animals or plants that make up our diets. The food we eat and the way we prepare the food can make a difference in the way we act and how healthy we are.

3   Sugar tastes good and makes our food sweet. Sugar gives us quick energy. After a while, though, sugar stops giving us energy and makes us feel sleepy instead. If we eat a lot of sugar, soon we move slowly. We are out of energy and we begin to be unfriendly to other people.

4   Meat is tasty and delicious. If we eat a lot of meat, chemicals build up in our body and can lead to heart attacks, strokes, and other diseases. It is important to limit the amount of meat in our food intake.

5   Food cooked in hot oil tastes wonderful. Frying food in oil or grease can put the same chemicals in our bodies as meat does. Cooking in the oven instead of the frying pan can cut down on the diseases caused by fried foods.

6   Doctors and nutritionists tell us that eating salads, fruit, vegetables, and grains will help us stay healthy. These are good foods for us and most people like their taste.

7   You will not become a cow if you eat a hamburger. You will not become an apple if you eat an apple. However, you will be healthier if you eat more apples and fewer hamburgers.

C. Circle **true** or **false** for each statement. Change the false sentences so they are true.

1. All foods are good for you.	TRUE	FALSE
2. Hamburgers contain some chemicals that are not good for people.	TRUE	FALSE
3. Nutritionists believe that people should eat less fruit.	TRUE	FALSE
4. Baked foods are less healthy than fried foods.	TRUE	FALSE
5. People should never eat sugar.	TRUE	FALSE

A. List all the foods you have eaten today.

Foods I Have Eaten Today

_____

_____

_____

_____

_____

B. Compare your list with a classmate.

C. List the ways you and your partner can eat a more healthy diet.

Ways to Eat a More Healthy Diet

_____ *Drink more water every day.* _____

_____

_____

_____

_____

A. Read the instructions for home care after surgery below.

B. Use the glossary on pages 98–103 to learn about new words.

🎧

Carter's Health Clinic
_____

DIRECTIONS FOR HOME CARE AFTER CLINIC SURGERY

Today's ___*stitches*___ for ___*cut finger*___ were successful. You will soon feel much better. Here are several important instructions for you to follow at home to make sure that you will heal quickly and maintain your good health.

1. If your doctor gave you a prescription, be sure to have it filled at a pharmacy and follow all the directions on the bottle.

2. Unless your doctor directed you to do so, do not change the bandage for the rest of the day.

3. Keep the bandage dry. You may take a bath or wash. Cover the bandage with plastic.

4. A bath or a sponge bath is better than a shower for now.

5. Rest for as long as your doctor tells you to. Avoid using the part of your body that was operated on.

6. Itching is part of the healing process. Avoid scratching the area of the operation.

7. Eat well balanced meals and drink extra amounts of water.

8. A small amount of bleeding may occur. If it does not stop, call the clinic for further instructions.

9. Your doctor or the clinic will call you this evening to check on your progress.

10. You may return to work when your doctor advises you to do so.

C. Write the correct instruction number next to each activity. Then circle **yes** if it's ok to do this activity or **no** if its's not ok.

	INSTRUCTION NUMBER	IS THIS ACTIVITY OK?	
1. Eat only ice cream.	_7_	YES	NO
2. Go out to a dance.	_____	YES	NO
3. Take a hot shower.	_____	YES	NO
4. Take the bandage off to wash.	_____	YES	NO
5. Drink a lot of water.	_____	YES	NO

A. On your own, think about the rules your family follows to stay healthy. Describe one practice in detail below.

A Healthy Living Practice

_____

_____

_____

B. Share your healthy living practice with a small group of your classmates.

C. With the members of your class, collect several of the best ideas to make a small book about healthy living practices. Design a cover for the book and think about how your class can make copies for everyone.

Vocabulary Review ★ ★ ★ ★ ★ ★ ★ ★ ★ ★ ★

Match the words on the left with their meanings on the right.

1. _E_ nutritionist   A. try not to do something

2. ____ tasty   B. seeds of plant used for food

3. ____ stroke   C. good to eat

4. ____ limit   D. get better; return to health

5. ____ grains   E̶. expert in healthy eating

6. ____ heal   F. sudden illness that makes it difficult to move or talk

7. ____ avoid   G. control the amount

CHAPTER **13**

LEARNING FOCUS

Content:
- ★ Recognizing advertising traps
- ★ Choosing ways to pay

Reading:
- ★ Interpreting claims
- ★ Letters of complaint

Language:
- ★ Conducting and graphing a survey
- ★ Writing a letter of complaint

Personal Finances:
Making Smart Choices

1 Talk About It

Discuss these questions with your class.

- ★ Where do you do most of your shopping?
- ★ How do you know how much to spend?
- ★ What do you do when people call you on the phone to sell something?

A. Work with partner. Conduct a survey of at least ten other students at your school. Ask them the three questions on the left side of the chart. Tally the number of responses in the spaces on the right side

1. How do you learn about the things you buy?	Newspaper ads	TV ads	Friends	Other
2. Do ads usually tell the truth about the things you buy?	Yes	No	Sometimes	Don't know
3. What can you do if you are not happy with something you buy?	Take it back	Keep it	Write a letter	Other

B. Choose one question and one set of answers you collected. Then make a bar graph to show how the students responded.

Question: _____?

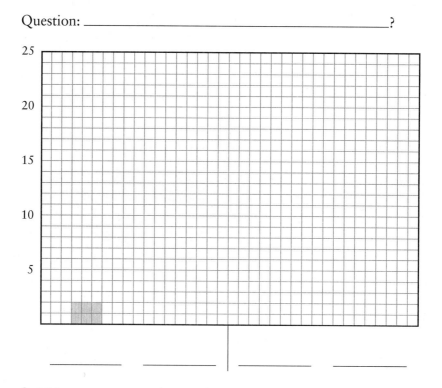

C. Write one sentence that explains what the graph shows. Read your sentence and present your graph to the class.

A. Read the newspaper advertisement for mattresses carefully. Find "traps" in the words, ways in which the store tries to make things sound better than they really are.

B. Use the glossary on pages 98–103 to learn about new words.

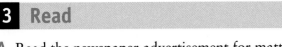

Going out of business!

Only 1.5% interest monthly.

Your credit is good with us, when qualified.

We **stand behind** our product.
No lower price in town this week.

Over twenty years in business.
Movie stars love this mattress.
Doctor-recommended.

We *selling at a loss* to move the merchandise. Only $235 takes this mattress home.

Hurry in before they're gone.

	Mattress	Box Spring
Twin	$235	$150
Double	$325	$175
Queen Size	$475	$200
King Size	$585	$250

Mattresses sold only in mattress-box spring sets.

C. Choose the best comment about each sentence from the advertisement.

1. Going out of business.
   A. This store is closing and the prices are low.
   B. The store wants to sell to more people.

2. Hurry in before they're gone.
   A. Prices will be higher soon.
   B. The store will not order more.

3. We are selling at a loss.
   A. The store will not make any profit from you.
   B. This is not true. The store always makes a profit from sales.

4. Only 1.5% interest monthly.
   A. This is a very low rate of interest.
   B. You are really paying almost 20% more because the rate is for a month, not a year.

5. Only $235 takes this mattress home.
   A. This is a very good deal.
   B. This is not true because you have to buy a whole set of two pieces.

A. Discuss the four different ways to buy things with a small group of your classmates. What do you think is the best way to pay? What other ways do you know?

Ways to pay	Cash	Credit	Check	Loan
Must have	money at the time of purchase	a credit card or store account	a checking account	good credit at a bank or lending institution
Must do		pay in full when the bill comes or make monthly payments plus interest	keep enough money in the bank and write a check	borrow money and pay it back plus interest

B. Read the list of things to buy. With your group, discuss the best way to pay for each thing. Give a reason for each choice.

	How to Pay	Why?
Shoes	*credit card*	*I don't carry enough cash.*
Food from the supermarket	_____	_____
New furniture	_____	_____
Gasoline	_____	_____
Used car	_____	_____
Hospital bill	_____	_____
Automobile insurance	_____	_____
Movie tickets	_____	_____

A. Read the letter from Robert Moises to the Talk Time Radio Company about the radio he bought.

B. Use the glossary on pages 98–103 to learn about new words.

1245 Blaine St.
West Brook, CA 94405
June 16, 2005

Talk Time Radio Co.
45 W. 36th Street
New York, New York 10015

Dear Sirs:

I bought one of your radios, model ST61, at Bargain City. It worked well for only one week. After that, I could not change the station. You can see from the enclosed receipt that I bought the radio on June 8 of this year.

I read the instructions on how to return the radio. I am sending you the broken radio and a copy of the receipt for $75.00 plus tax. I had to pay $5.00 postage to send you the radio.

Please repair the radio and return it to me. If you can't repair it, I want a new one. You can send the radio to the address above.

Thank you for your help.

Yours truly,

Robert Moises

enc.

C. Write short answers to the questions below.

EXAMPLE: What is wrong with the radio?

He can't change the station.

1. Where does Robert Moises live?

   _____

2. Where did he buy the radio?

   _____

3. What is the purpose of the letter?

   _____

4. What does Robert want if the company is not able to repair the radio?

   _____

5. How does Robert end the letter?

   _____

A. Work with a group of two other classmates. Read about Martin Bolton's problem below. Then follow the instructions to write a letter of complaint from Martin to the hotel manager.

> Martin Bolton had a very big party at a big hotel in your city. He paid the hotel $50.00 per person for the dinner. The next day, James Richards, one of his friends, told Martin that he did not get the meal at the party. James asked the waiter to bring him his food, but the waiter never brought it. James did not want to make trouble at the party, but he wanted Martin to know that one meal was not served. Later Martin found out that two other friends did not get their food.

1. Make up a name and address for the hotel and an address for Martin Bolton.
2. Look carefully at the letter on page 77 to know where to put the addresses, the date, and other parts of the letter.
3. Each member of your group will write one paragraph. Follow this model:
   a. In paragraph 1, tell what the problem is.
   b. In paragraph 2, explain how much Martin had paid and how many meals should have been served.
   c. In paragraph 3, tell the manager what Martin wants the hotel to do to fix the problem

4. Close the letter in a friendly manner.

B. Share your letter with other groups in the class.

Vocabulary Review ★ ★ ★ ★ ★ ★ ★ ★ ★ ★ ★ ★

Match the words on the left with their meanings on the right.

1. _E_ consumer   A. paper that shows you bought something

2. ____ credit   B. telling why you don't like something

3. ____ interest   C. smallest amount of money you must pay each month

4. ____ minimum payment   D. to put inside

5. ____ complaint   E. person who buys and uses items

6. ____ receipt   F. agreement to pay later

7. ____ enclose   G. extra money you pay to be allowed to pay later

CHAPTER **14**

LEARNING FOCUS

Content:
- ★ Family budgeting
- ★ Using credit

Reading:
- ★ Reading for general ideas
- ★ Interpreting information on fliers

Language:
- ★ Reporting quantitative information
- ★ Using conversation strategies

Personal Finances:
Staying Out of Debt

1 Talk About It

"And in only 162 payments, this little baby is yours."

Discuss these questions with your class.

- ★ What is happening in the picture?
- ★ Do you buy things from door-to-door salespeople? Why or why not?
- ★ What are some of the dangers of using credit cards?

A. Work with a partner. Take turns asking and answering questions about the information in the chart. Use a calculator if you wish.

EXAMPLE: *How much do the Wilsons save every month?*
They save 5% of their income. That's about $145.

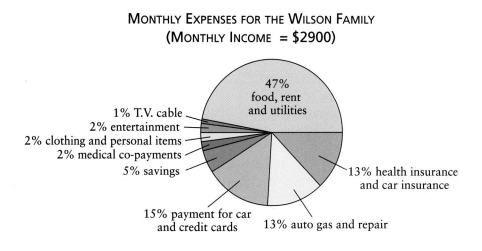

MONTHLY EXPENSES FOR THE WILSON FAMILY
(MONTHLY INCOME = $2900)

1% T.V. cable
2% entertainment
2% clothing and personal items
2% medical co-payments
5% savings

47% food, rent and utilities

13% health insurance and car insurance

15% payment for car and credit cards

13% auto gas and repair

B. Join another set of partners to form a small group. Read the following situation and answer the question at the end.

> The Wilsons want to take a trip to see their relatives for a holiday. The airplane tickets will cost $1500 and they need $500 more for expenses. They plan to save the money over several months. They will use the money from their savings.
>
> How long will it take the Wilson family to save enough money?
>
> _____

C. Discuss the steps your group took to reach your answer and report to the class.

A. Read the newspaper story about using credit cards. Look for the main ideas and for the details.

B. Use the glossary on pages 98–103 to learn about new words.

Let the Buyer Beware

1   *Washington, D.C.* The old Latin saying *caveat emptor* is still true according to a government report released this week. The Commerce Department said that the phrase, which means "let the buyer beware," is a warning to users of credit.

2   In the United States, many millions of people are in trouble for using credit cards in the wrong way. Credit cards can cost consumers more money than they save. Typically, the store has to pay the credit card company about 5% of the cost of the item.

3   The stores include the 5% in the cost of the things they sell. They see credit as an easy way for people to buy, so they are happy to pay a little extra to get customers. However, they will charge more for everything they sell to get back the money it costs to accept credit cards.

4   Credit card companies also charge credit card users. First, they often ask credit card holders to pay an annual fee. Then, the credit card companies charge more money if the credit card bill is not fully paid at the end of each month. The company adds a finance charge to any amount that is owed at the end of the month. If the credit card holder lets the amount stay for a year, the interest can add up to more than 25%. If a person buys clothes at a 10% off sale, and does not pay the bill at the end of the month, the amount to be paid will be more than the 10% savings. The store wins, the credit card company wins, and the buyer loses.

5   Buyers need to be aware of how they use credit cards. The amount of the bill needs to be paid at the end of each month. If not, the cost for the card user will be very high. *Caveat emptor* to all of us.

C. Complete each sentence with the best ending.

1. This newspaper story is mostly about _____ .
   A. buying good things
   B. paying for things you buy
   C. using credit cards
   D. paying your credit card bills

2. The stores that take credit cards have to _____ .
   A. charge more money
   B. pay the credit card holder
   C. sell for less money
   D. advertise more

3. *Caveat emptor* is a warning in Latin to _____ .
   A. pay less
   B. be careful when buying something
   C. never use credit
   D. throw away your credit cards

4. A careful shopper _____ .
   A. never buys anything
   B. buys more than is needed
   C. pays all of the credit card bill each month
   D. pays a finance charge each month

A. Look over the list of sample conversation strategies below.

STRATEGIES	WHAT THEY MEAN
I agree.	You think the same thing as someone else.
You may be right, but I think . . .	You want to tell the speaker a different idea.
That's not the only way.	You think there is a different idea that is just as good or better.
I understand what you are saying.	You heard another person's ideas, but you may not agree.
I understand what you are saying, but I see it differently.	You heard the other person's ideas, but you definitely do not agree and now you want to tell what you think.

B. Work with a partner. Choose or think of a polite conversation strategy to express the following opinions. Then make up a short conversation to practice each strategy.

1. That's a silly idea.

2. I am right and you are wrong.

3. You told your idea well.

4. I disagree and want to tell my idea.

5. We are both right.

    EXAMPLE: A: *Credit cards are a great way to pay for everything.*

                      B: *I understand what you're saying, but I think it's better to pay cash.*

A. Read the following flier about getting help with credit problems. As you read, think about whether it is a good idea.

B. Use the glossary on pages 98–103 to learn about new words.

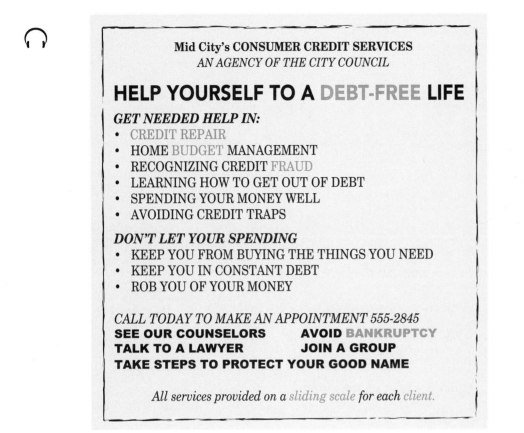

Mid City's **CONSUMER CREDIT SERVICES**
AN AGENCY OF THE CITY COUNCIL

HELP YOURSELF TO A DEBT-FREE LIFE

GET NEEDED HELP IN:
- CREDIT REPAIR
- HOME BUDGET MANAGEMENT
- RECOGNIZING CREDIT FRAUD
- LEARNING HOW TO GET OUT OF DEBT
- SPENDING YOUR MONEY WELL
- AVOIDING CREDIT TRAPS

DON'T LET YOUR SPENDING
- KEEP YOU FROM BUYING THE THINGS YOU NEED
- KEEP YOU IN CONSTANT DEBT
- ROB YOU OF YOUR MONEY

CALL TODAY TO MAKE AN APPOINTMENT 555-2845

SEE OUR COUNSELORS	**AVOID BANKRUPTCY**
TALK TO A LAWYER	**JOIN A GROUP**
TAKE STEPS TO PROTECT YOUR GOOD NAME	

All services provided on a sliding scale for each client.

C. Discuss these questions with a partner. Decide on one answer for each question.

EXAMPLE: Who should use Consumer Credit Services?

People who have problems with debt and budgets

1. Do all people pay the same amount to use Consumer Credit Services? Why?

2. What can Consumer Credit Services do to help people?

3. How can you "protect your good name"?

4. Why do some people need this service?

6 Group Work

A. Work with a small group of your classmates. Read the information about the Danier family's finances in the box below.

> Mr. and Mrs. Danier bring home about $3,200 each month. They have one child. They want to have another baby, and they live in an apartment. They want to have a house of their own. They need to save about $15,000 for a down payment to get a house. They have already saved $5,000.

B. Decide how much money they can spend each month and still save enough money to buy a house in a reasonable time.

C. Share your plan for the Daniers with the rest of the class.

Vocabulary Review ★ ★ ★ ★ ★ ★ ★ ★ ★ ★

Match the words on the left with their meanings on the right.

1. __C__ Latin   A. illegal tricks or lies to get money
2. _____ annual fee   B. to know about
3. _____ finance charge   C. language of ancient Rome
4. _____ debt free   D. money paid for service each year
5. _____ fraud   E. percentage added to a monthly bill
6. _____ be aware of   F. person receiving a service
7. _____ client   G. legally unable to pay debts
8. _____ bankruptcy   H. not owing any money

Small Claims:
Looking for Solutions

1 Talk About It

Discuss these questions with your class.

★ What is happening in the picture?

★ Who will pay for the broken window?

★ What happens if somebody doesn't want to pay?

A. Work with partner. Read each of the following situations. For each one, state both the problem and the solution.

Example:

Mr. Jones bought a new dog. It was very young. Every night the dog barked and barked. The neighbors had trouble sleeping. One of the neighbors came to Mr. Jones's house and asked him to stop the dog's barking. Mr. Jones said that he would try. The dog continued to bark all night every night.

Problem: *The dog kept everyone awake all night.*

Solution: *Mr. Jones has to try harder or get rid of the dog.*

Mrs. Torres bought a new television at the store. When she got home, she found that the TV did not work. She took it back and the store gave her a new one. It did not work either. When she took it back, she wanted her money back. The manager of the store said that the store would give her another television but would not give her the money back.

Problem: _____

Solution: _____

My friend Paul took his car to be fixed by a mechanic. The mechanic told him that he had to have a new fuel pump and charged him $250 to replace the old fuel pump. Paul got the car back later that day. When he drove the car, it had the same problem. Paul took the car back to the mechanic. The mechanic said that the car had a different problem and he could fix that problem for another $150.

Problem: _____

Solution: _____

A. Read about small claims courts in the following passage.

B. Use the glossary on pages 98–103 to learn about new words.

A Court for All the People

1   When companies and people cannot solve big problems by themselves, there are **lawyers** and courts to help them. What about you and me? How can we decide who should pay or who is wrong?

2   Some states have small claims courts where people can tell their stories to a judge. The judge will decide who is right in each case. These cases are limited in the amount of money people can claim. In some states the amount is $5,000 or less.

3   There are no lawyers to **represent** the two sides in small claims court. The people tell their story to a judge by themselves. Each side shows its **evidence** to tell who was right and who was wrong. The judge listens to both sides and decides who was correct according to the law. Any person can go to court in a small claims court. It is easy to start a **lawsuit** and it is easy to present your case. The person who brings the lawsuit is the plaintiff, and the person who is accused of doing something wrong is the defendant.

4   During the **trial**, the plaintiff tells the story of what happened and why the defendant should pay. The plaintiff shows the judge evidence of what happened. The evidence may be a contract, pictures, bills, or anything that shows how much is owed or what took place. The defendant can show evidence, too.

5   The small claims court judge knows the law. After hearing what both sides have to say, the judge makes a decision. If the plaintiff is right, the defendant has to pay. If the plaintiff does not prove the defendant is wrong, then the defendant does not have to pay anything. Because small claims courts are easy to use and because people do not need to hire lawyers, they are sometimes called "courts for all the people."

C. Choose which sentences are **true** and which are **false.** Change the false sentences so they are true.

1. You need to talk to a lawyer to use the small claims court.   TRUE   FALSE

2. The idea of small claims court is to decide who is right and who is wrong in arguments about money.   TRUE   FALSE

3. It takes many years to get a decision from a small claims court.   TRUE   FALSE

4. Only the plaintiff can show evidence to the judge.   TRUE   FALSE

5. A lawyer decides who is right and who is wrong in small claims court.   TRUE   FALSE

4 Discuss

A. Tell a partner about a problem you have had. For example, it can be a problem with another person or with an employer, a landlord, or a business. Use these questions as guidelines to tell your story.

1. What happened to cause the problem?

2. What was the problem?

3. How did the problem end?

B. As you listen to your partner, take notes that will help you remember the story.

C. Get together with another pair of your classmates. Tell the group your partner's story.

5 Read More

A. Discuss the following picture with the the class. What do you think is about to happen?

B. Read the following story. Try to remember the important facts.

C. Use the glossary on pages 98–103 to learn about new words.

A Day in Small Claims Court

1 It was small claims court day in the county court house. A regular judge was sitting in her chair. In front of her were two tables. A person sat at each table. One man was dressed in a short-sleeved shirt because it was a warm summer day. The other man wore work clothes.

2 "Good morning," said the judge. "We are here to hear Small Claims Case number 12-8376. Mr. Winslow versus Mr. Tomlon. Which one of you is Mr. Winslow?"

3 "I am," said the man in the short-sleeved shirt.

4 "You are the plaintiff in this case. And you must be Mr. Tomlon. You are the defendant in the case," the judge said. "Now, Mr. Winslow, you must tell the story of what happened. If you have any evidence for your story, you must show it to me. Mr. Tomlon, you and I will listen very carefully. If you disagree with Mr. Winslow, don't say anything now. You will get a chance to talk later. Mr. Winslow, please begin."

5 "Well, **your honor**, it began a few months ago when my family and I were at the park. We were watching my daughter play soccer. We were standing near our field. Another soccer ball came past us from behind. Mr. Tomlon was running after the ball. He pushed my little son as he ran past us. My son fell down and hurt his arm. Mr. Tomlon said he was sorry, but he didn't stop to help.

6 "My little son was crying and crying. We took him to the clinic near the park. They took an X-ray and saw that his arm was broken. The doctor put the arm in a cast and gave us a prescription for some medicine. The doctor charged us $1,500. The prescription cost $50.00 at the pharmacy. I wrote a letter to Mr. Tomlon to ask him to pay us the money. He never gave us any."

7 The judged asked the plaintiff some questions. "Do you have any evidence of what you told me? Do you know that this is the person who pushed your little son?"

8 Mr. Winslow showed the judge the bill from the clinic. He showed her the receipt from the pharmacy, and he showed the judge the letter he had written to Mr. Tomlon. Mr. Winslow said that he knows Mr. Tomlon because he sees him in the neighborhood.

9 "Thank you," said the judge. "Now, Mr. Tomlon. You can tell us what you say happened.

10 "Well," began Mr. Tomlon, "This little jerk and his family . . ."

11 "Stop there," the judge said in an angry voice, "We will all talk to each other with respect at all times. I will not tell anybody this again. You will not help your case by being **rude**."

12 "I'm sorry, your honor. But this man and his family were running up and down the side of the field. They were not looking at the other people in the park. I was running after the ball when the little boy ran into me. I got my ball from the field, and then I saw that the boy

was on the ground. I did not mean to hurt him. It was an accident. Besides, Mr. Winslow has health insurance to pay for the clinic."

13 "Is that true, Mr. Winslow? Did you get some money from your insurance company to pay for your medical bills?" the judge asked.

14 "Yes, your honor. I had to pay for the first $200 of the clinic bill. The insurance company paid for part of the rest," answered Mr. Winslow.

15 "How much did they give you?" the judge wanted to know.

16 "The insurance company sent me a check for $875.00. They did not pay for the pharmacy bill at all."

17 "I see," said the judge. "Well, I am ready to make my decision. I have heard that the Winslow family was watching a soccer game in a normal manner. Mr. Tomlon, an adult man, was running outside of a soccer field. While he did not mean to hurt anybody, he did. He should have to pay for any damage he caused. However, since Mr. Winslow's insurance company has already paid for some of the costs, Mr. Tomlon needs to pay the amount that the insurance did not pay. I **order** Mr. Tomlon to pay a total of $675 to Mr. Winslow. Case number 12-8376 is finished and I am ready to hear the next case."

6 Group Work

A. Re-read the story aloud with a small group of your classmates. Each one of you can take a different part in the reading (one can be the narrator, one the judge, and so on).

B. With your group, discuss the judge's decision. Was the amount of money Mr. Tomlon had to pay fair? Report your conclusion to the class.

Vocabulary Review ★ ★ ★ ★ ★ ★ ★ ★ ★ ★ ★ ★

Match the words on the left with their meanings on the right.

1. __F__ plaintiff   A. proof of the facts to show the judge

2. _____ defendant   B. person who helps people with the laws

3. _____ judge   C. person who decides a case in a court

4. _____ lawsuit   D. formal complaint made in a court of law

5. _____ lawyer   E. person accused of doing something wrong

6. _____ evidence   F. person who brings a case to court

7. _____ rude   G. very impolite; disrespectful

CHAPTER **16**

LEARNING FOCUS

Content:

* Organizing and evaluating evidence
* Presenting evidence

Reading:

* Reading for categories of information
* Recognizing logical thinking

Language:

* Distinguishing facts from opinions
* Supporting opinions

Small Claims:
Thinking Clearly

1 **Talk About It**

Discuss these questions with your class.

* What's the problem in the picture?

* Do you think the bus driver and the other drivers will tell the same story about the accident?

* Do you sometimes see a problem differently from a friend or relative? Tell about it.

* Who is a good person to settle an argument between friends?

A. Work with partner. Decide if each of the following statements is a fact or an opinion. If it is a fact, tell what kind of evidence would prove that it is true.

EXAMPLE: The stone put a dent in my car. (FACT) OPINION

Proof: *A photo of the dent and the stone*

1. That was the best pie I ever tasted. FACT OPINION

_____

2. The hospital charged my family $2,000 for one day. FACT OPINION

_____

3. I went to the baseball game on that day. I wasn't at the beach. FACT OPINION

_____

4. Many people saw him throw the brick at the window. FACT OPINION

_____

5. Nobody liked the movie that night. FACT OPINION

_____

6. Cake is the best dessert for a big party. FACT OPINION

_____

7. I worked ten hours and only received money for eight hours. FACT OPINION

_____

B. Present your evidence to the class. Decide who has the best evidence for each fact.

3 **Read** ★

A. Different types of admissible evidence include a written contract, a photo of a dent on a car, a broken watch, a hospital bill, a time card showing days absent, a paid check, and so on. Discuss each type with your class.

B. Read about the different kinds of evidence used in court cases in the following passage.

C. Use the glossary on pages 98–103 to learn about new words.

Good Evidence Tells the Story

1   In small claims court, both the plaintiff and the defendant tell their stories. Naturally, each tells the story to show that his or her side is correct. What helps the judge decide who is right? Both sides can be nice people. Both sides can strongly believe that they are correct. The judge needs to look at facts to see who is correct and who is not correct under the law.

2   Each side shows evidence to prove its case. For example, if one side says that a car was damaged, photographs can show the damage. A bill for the repair of the car can show what was fixed and what the damage was. The bill will also show how much it cost to repair the car.

3   Photographs are clear evidence to show the judge damage to a person's car or home. They can also show where events happened. Usually, there is not a photograph of an event when it happened. In a traffic accident, there might be a photograph of the damage to both cars, but it would be unusual to have a picture of the two cars actually hitting each other.

4   Documents such as bills, checks, and receipts can show a connection between a story and what really happened. If a person says that three days of work were lost, a copy of a paycheck can show what days they were. If a person says that it cost money to buy a new item that was broken, the receipt for the item can show how much it cost. If a homeowner says a workman promised to paint a room, a written contract will show the details of the promise. If a defendant says the bills were paid, a copy of the check cashed by the plaintiff will show that the bill was paid.

5   People can be good evidence. A person who actually saw and heard what happened is a witness. The witness must know the facts well enough to answer questions from the judge or the other side in the case. Both plaintiffs and defendants can use the evidence of witnesses.

6   Sometimes the defendant or the plaintiff brings an item to the courtroom. For example, if the question has to do with a watch, the plaintiff or the defendant can bring the actual watch.

7   By bringing evidence into a court, a plaintiff or a defendant can try to convince the judge that a story is correct.

D. Give examples of what you would use these pieces of evidence to prove.
For example, a photograph would prove damage to a car.

a photograph	a calendar
a receipt	an airplane ticket
a paid check	a broken pair of glasses

A. With a partner, discuss the kinds of evidence that would prove each of these statements.

Example: "That man grabbed my purse and ran away with it."

Evidence: *a witness who saw it happen, film from a*

surveillance camera

1. "That car backed into my bicycle."

_____

2. "He didn't paint my house the color that I wanted."

_____

3. "I paid him all the money already."

_____

4. "She stood in the street and yelled bad names at me."

_____

5. "I fixed the refrigerator and it worked perfectly."

_____

B. Think of a complaint that a plaintiff might bring to small claims court. With your partner, write a statement that summarizes the complaint. Describe the type of evidence that would prove it.

_____

_____

_____

_____

_____

_____

_____

_____

_____

_____

_____

_____

_____

A. Read the advice about getting ready to go to small claims court.

B. Use the glossary on pages 98–103 to learn about new words.

Getting Ready to Go to Court

1   When a case is filed at a small claims court, the court employees will help to make all the **arrangements** for the trial.

2   What happens in the trial is up to the plaintiff and the defendant. The side that wins is often the side that is best prepared. The plaintiff and the defendant have to be ready to tell the judge what happened and have the proof ready to show the judge.

3   Good evidence on both sides can be documents, witnesses, photographs, or the actual items in question. To tell their stories, the plaintiffs have to put the evidence in order and present the story in a **logical** way. The best way to tell what happened is in the order in which it happened. As the story is told, people use the evidence to prove the story. Usually, each side tries to think of what the other side might say and tell the judge its own ideas or show evidence to the judge.

4   Before the sides go to court, they should practice what they will say. They want to make sure that they **submit** all the evidence so that the judge can understand their story. They have to think about what evidence to show and when to show it. They have to think about what words to use and how to say them.

5   In the court, the people must stand to talk to the judge. They should try to look their best. Men should wear a long-sleeved shirt and a tie. Women should wear business clothes. Looking good will not win a case, but it won't hurt.

6   Small claims court is a place for everybody. You do not have to know a lawyer or be a lawyer to make your case, but it does help to prepare well. When there is no other peaceful way to settle a problem, let the judge help you.

C. Add details to these ideas about going to small claims court.

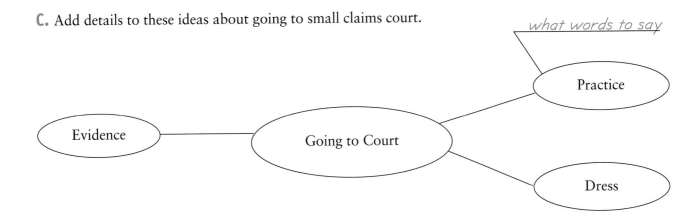

what words to say

Evidence — Going to Court — Practice — Dress

6 Group Work

A. Work with a small group of your classmates to prepare this case for small claims court.

> Bob Bright bought an expensive ring for his girlfriend, Lois. She promised that she was going to marry him. Then Lois met Tom. Lois decided that she loved Tom more and wanted to marry him. Bob wanted Lois to give him the ring back, but Lois said that it belonged to her. Bob wants $3,000 or the ring.

B. Choose someone from your group to present Bob's case for the class.

Vocabulary Review ★ ★ ★ ★ ★ ★ ★ ★ ★ ★ ★ ★

Match the words on the left with their meanings on the right.

1. _E_ event

2. ___ document

3. ___ witness

4. ___ item

5. ___ convince

6. ___ logical

7. ___ arrangements

A. according to a pattern of thinking

B. preparations

C. a person who sees and hears an event

D. make someone agree with you

E. something that happens

F. a paper that shows information

G. a thing

Appendices

Appendix A

Glossary

The numbers in parentheses are the chapters in which the terms appear.

★ A ★

absence note	letter from a parent that tells why a student was not in school. (10)
access	ability to use or receive a thing or a service. (5)
accompany	to go with a person. (6)
according to	as somebody told you. *According to* the Channel 11 news, it's going to rain today. (14)
advance permission	an O.K. to do something before the time. (5)
annual fee	an amount of money you pay every year. (14)
appliances	electrical machines used in the home, for example, a refrigerator, a dishwasher, a toaster. (5)
appointment	a time to meet. (10)
arrangements	preparations for an event. (16)
attract	to make people want to go somewhere or look at something. (4)
avoid	to try *not* to do something. (12)

★ B ★

bankruptcy	not having enough money to pay what you owe. (14)
be aware of	to know about. (14)
benefits	non-money payment for work. Health insurance is a *benefit* at some jobs. (8)
budget	a plan to use money. (14)

★ C ★

candidate	person who wants to be elected. (1)
certain circumstances	special times or conditions. (10)
chemical	a substance made of an element or combination of elements. Salt is made up of the *chemicals* sodium and chlorine. (127)
citizen	a person who belongs to a country. My cousin is a *citizen* of Mexico. (1)
client	person receiving a professional service. (14)
commercial	advertisement on radio or television. (4)
complain	to tell about a problem. (5)
compulsory education	school attendance required by law. (9)
concerned	worried. (5)
contain	to have inside. My wallet *contains* three one-dollar bills. (4)
contract	a written agreement. (7)
cooperate	to work together. (2)
co-payment	money paid for health care in addition to insurance. (11)
counselor	person at school who helps students choose classes. (10)
credit repair	help with a credit problem. (14)

★ D ★

debt free	owing no money to anyone. (14)
deduction	amount of money taken out of a paycheck. (7)
delivery	package arriving by mail or special truck. (6)
democracy	system of government in which all citizens can vote. (2)
depend on	to change because of other events. The clothes we wear *depend on* the weather. (4)
diet	the food people normally eat. (12)
document	paper that shows information. (16)

★ E ★

election	a time to make choices for an office, for example, mayor or president. (1)
electronic	using electricity to send information instead of using it for power, for example, cell phones, computers, digital cameras. (3)
eligible	able to receive a benefit. (8)
enclose	to put inside. (13)
enforce	to make someone obey a rule or law. (5)

event	something that happens. (16)
evidence	proof of the facts to show a judge. (15)

★ F ★

finance charge	extra money you pay for using credit. (14)
fraud	illegal tricks or lies to get money. (14)

★ G ★

government clinic	medical center run by the government. (11)
government	a system for making laws and enforcing them. (1)

★ H ★

heal	to get better. (12)

★ I ★

illness	sickness, disease. (11)
immediate family	close relatives, such as mother, father, daughter, or son. (10)
immediately	without delay. (8)
income tax	tax on the money you make at work. (7)
item	a thing. (16)

★ L ★

landlord	person who owns rental property. (5)
Latin	language of ancient Rome. (14)
laundry facilities	a place to wash and dry clothes. (5)
laws	a government's rules. (1)
lawsuit	formal complaint made in a court of law. (15)
lawyer	person who helps people understand the law. (15)
legal assistance	help from a lawyer or group of lawyers. (7)
lessee	renter, person or family who agree to rent an apartment or other property for a period of time. (6)
lessor	landlord, person or company that rents or leases property to tenants. (6)
let the buyer beware	a customer should be always be very careful. (14)

| limit | to control the amount. (12) |
| logical | according to a clear pattern of thinking. (16) |

★ M ★

maintain	to keep in good working condition. (12)
manager	person in charge of a property. (6)
Medicare	federal program that helps pay for health care for people over the age of 65. (7)
minimum wage	smallest amount an employer can pay per hour. (7)
minor	below the legal age of an adult. (6)
mix	to put together, combine. (4)

★ N ★

national	for all of the country. (9)
notice	a letter with information. (6)
nutritionist	expert in healthy eating. (12)

★ O ★

obviously	in a way that is easy to understand. (12)
occupant	person who lives in a room, house, or apartment. (6)
occur	to happen. (12)
open house	time for parents to visit teachers and classrooms. (10)
order	to give a command. (15)
ordinance	law or rule made by a government, especially a city government. (6)
overtime	extra time worked over the usual number of hours. (7)
owe	to have to pay money to someone. (14)

★ P ★

particular	one special out of many (possibilities). (4)
physician	medical doctor. (11)
policy	set of rules for a school, company, or government. (10)
post high school	after high school. (10)
premises	land and the buildings on it. (6)

premium	money you pay for insurance. (8)
prescription	a paper with the names of drugs a doctor wants you to take. (12)
principal	manager of a school. (10)
private doctor	doctor who is not part of a large organization. (11)
property	things you own: furniture, land, clothes, a building. (6)

★ R ★

reason	why things happen. (2)
recommend	to say good things about someone or something. (11)
reimbursement	money paid back by an insurance company to a patient. (11)
religious holiday	day to celebrate an important event in a religion, for example, Three Kings' Day, Muslim New Year, Yom Kippur, Full Moon Festival. (10)
report card	paper that tells how a student is doing in school. (10)
represent	to speak for another person. (15)
require	to make a person do something. (10)
respect	to think a person or idea is important. (2)
responsible	in charge of, accountable for. (10)
return	to take or send something back. (13)
roommate	person who shares a room or apartment but is not a relative. (5)
rude	not polite. (15)

★ S ★

schedule	to plan for something to happen at a specific time. (10)
security deposit	money paid to a landlord at the beginning of the rental period. This money is returned at the end of the period if there is no damage to the property. (5)
sell at a loss	sell something for less money than you bought it for. (13)
service	a doctor's work. (11)
sliding scale	payment based on the money you earn. (14)
Social Security	government program that helps people when they retire or are not able to work. (7)
specialized	given by a medical doctor trained in a special type of care, for example, treatment of eyes, feet, or skin. (11)
spouse	the person you marry, a husband or wife. (8)
stand behind	believe something is good, support it. (13)

statute	law made by a government, usually a state government or the federal government. (6)
submit	to send. (16)
superintendent	manager of a school system. (10)
supervisor	your boss at work. (8)

★ T ★

tax	money paid to a government. (11)
tenant	person who rents a place to live. (5)
trial	legal process to find out if someone owes money or has committed a crime. (15)
trust	to believe that someone is telling the truth. I trust what my friends tell me. (4)

★ U ★

unemployment insurance	program that gives money to people who lose their jobs. (7)
union dues	money you pay for membership in a labor union. (7)
unite	act together. (5)

★ V ★

visual	able to be seen. (3)

★ W ★

witness	person who has seen or heard evidence. (16)
work by the piece	to get paid on the basis of how much work you complete. (7)

★ Y ★

your honor	respectful words used to speak to a judge in a court of law. (15)

Appendix B

100 Citizenship Questions

Applicants for U.S. citizenship are asked some of these 100 questions during their citizenship test. You can test yourself by covering the answers and attempting to answer them.

Questions	Answers
1. What are the colors of our flag?	Red, white, and blue.
2. How many stars are there in our flag?	50.
3. What color are the stars on our flag?	White.
4. What do the stars on the flag mean?	There is one star for each state in the Union.
5. How many stripes are there in the flag?	13.
6. What color are the stripes?	Red and white.
7. What do the stripes on the flag mean?	They represent the original 13 states.
8. How many states are there in the Union?	50.
9. What is the 4th of July?	Independence Day.
10. What is the date of Independence Day?	July 4th.
11. Independence from whom?	England.
12. What country did we fight during the Revolutionary War?	England.
13. Who was the first president of the United States?	George Washington.
14. Who is the president of the United States today?	_____
15. Who is the vice president of the United States today?	_____
16. Who elects the president of the United States?	The Electoral College.

17.	Who becomes president of the United States if the president should die?	The vice president.
18.	For how long do we elect the president?	Four years.
19.	What is the Constitution?	The supreme law of the land.
20.	Can the Constitution be changed?	Yes.
21.	What do we call a change to the Constitution?	An amendment.
22.	How many changes or amendments are there to the Constitution?	27.
23.	How many branches are there in our government?	Three.
24.	What are the three branches of our government?	Legislative, executive, and judiciary.
25.	What is the legislative branch of our government?	Congress.
26.	Who makes the laws in the United States?	Congress.
27.	What is the Congress?	The Senate and the House of Representatives.
28.	What are the duties of Congress?	To make laws.
29.	Who elects Congress?	The people.
30.	How many senators are there in Congress?	100.
31.	Can you name the two senators from your state?	_____
32.	For how long do we elect each senator?	Six years.
33.	How many representatives are there in Congress?	435.
34.	For how long do we elect the representatives?	Two years.
35.	What is the executive branch of our government?	The president, cabinet, and departments under the cabinet members.
36.	What is the judiciary branch of our government?	The Supreme Court.
37.	What are the duties of the Supreme Court?	To interpret laws.
38.	What is the supreme law of the United States?	The Constitution.
39.	What is the Bill of Rights?	The first ten amendments to the Constitution.
40.	What is the capital of your state?	_____
41.	Who is the current governor of your state?	_____
42.	Who becomes president of the United States if the president and the vice president should die?	The speaker of the House of Representatives.
43.	Who is the chief justice of the Supreme Court?	_____
44.	Can you name the 13 original states?	Delaware, Pennsylvania, New Jersey, Georgia, Connecticut, Massachusetts, Maryland, South Carolina, New Hampshire, Virginia, New York, North Carolina, and Rhode Island.
45.	Who said, "Give me liberty or give me death"?	Patrick Henry.

46.	Which countries were our enemies during World War II?	Germany, Italy, and Japan.
47.	What are the 49th and 50th states of the Union?	Hawaii (49th) and Alaska (50th).
48.	How many terms can the President serve?	Two.
49.	Who was Martin Luther King, Jr.?	A civil rights leader.
50.	Who is the head of your local government?	_____
51.	According to the Constitution, a person must meet certain requirements in order to be eligible to become president. Name one of these requirements.	A person must be a natural-born citizen of the United States. A person must be at least 35 years old. A person must have lived in the United States for at least 14 years.
52.	Why are there 100 senators in the Senate?	There are two from each state.
53.	Who selects the Supreme Court justices?	The president appoints them.
54.	How many Supreme Court justices are there?	Nine.
55.	Why did the Pilgrims come to America?	For religious freedom.
56.	What is the head executive of a state government called?	Governor.
57.	What is the head executive of a city government called?	Mayor.
58.	What holiday was celebrated for the first time by the American colonists?	Thanksgiving.
59.	Who was the main writer of the Declaration of Independence?	Thomas Jefferson.
60.	When was the Declaration of Independence adopted?	July 4, 1776.
61.	What is the basic belief of the Declaration of Independence?	That all men (=people) are created equal.
62.	What is the national anthem of the United States?	"The Star-Spangled Banner."
63.	Who wrote *The Star-Spangled Banner*?	Francis Scott Key.
64.	Where does freedom of speech come from?	The Bill of Rights.
65.	What is the minimum voting age in the United States?	18.
66.	Who signs bills into law?	The president.
67.	What is the highest court in the United States?	The Supreme Court.
68.	Who was the president during the Civil War?	Abraham Lincoln.
69.	What did the Emancipation Proclamation do?	It freed many slaves.

70. What special group advises the president?	The Cabinet.
71. Which president is called the "the father of our country"?	George Washington.
72. What Immigration and Naturalization Service form is used to apply to become a naturalized citizen?	Form N-400 (Application to File Petition for Naturalization).
73. Who helped the Pilgrims in America?	The American Indians (Native Americans).
74. What is the name of the ship that brought the Pilgrims to America?	The *Mayflower*.
75. What were the 13 original states of the United States called?	Colonies.
76. Name three rights or freedoms guaranteed by the Bill of Rights.	Freedom of speech Freedom of the press Freedom of religion Freedom of assembly The right to bear arms (own a gun) The government cannot force people to keep soldiers in their house during peacetime. The government needs a warrant to search or take a person's property. A person may not be tried twice for the same crime and does not have to testify against him/herself. The right to a trial and the right to a lawyer The right to a trial by jury Freedom from excessive or unreasonable fines or cruel and unusual punishment.
77. Who has the power to declare war?	Congress.
78. What kind of government does the United States have?	A democratic form of government/ A representative form of government/ The United States is a republic.
79. Which president freed the slaves?	Abraham Lincoln.
80. In what year was the Constitution written?	1787.
81. What are the first ten amendments to the Constitution called?	The Bill of Rights.
82. Name one purpose of the United Nations.	For countries to discuss and try to resolve world problems; to provide economic aid to many countries.
83. Where does Congress meet?	In the Capitol in Washington, D.C.
84. Whose rights are guaranteed by the Constitution and the Bill of Rights?	Everyone's (citizens and non-citizens living in United States).

85.	What is the introduction to the Constitution called?	The Preamble.
86.	Name one benefit of being a citizen of the United States.	Obtain federal government jobs Travel with U.S. passport Petition for close relatives to come to the United States to live.
87.	What is the most important right granted to U.S. citizens?	The right to vote.
88.	What is the United States Capitol?	The place where Congress meets.
89.	What is the White House?	The president's official home.
90.	Where is the White House located?	1600 Pennsylvania Ave. Northwest, Washington, D.C.
91.	What is the name of the president's official home?	The White House.
92.	Name one right guaranteed by the first amendment.	Freedom of speech, press, religion, assembly, and requesting change of the government.
93.	Who is the commander-in-chief of the U.S. military?	The president.
94.	Which president was the first commander-in-chief of the U.S. military?	George Washington.
95.	In what month do we vote for the president?	November.
96.	In what month is the new president inaugurated?	January.
97.	How many times may a senator be re-elected?	There is no limit.
98.	How many times may a congressman or congresswoman be re-elected?	There is no limit.
99.	What are the two major political parties in the United States today?	Democratic and Republican.
100.	How many states are there in the United States today?	50.

Appendix C

American Songs and Pledges

America the Beautiful

O beautiful for spacious skies,
for amber waves of grain,
For purple mountain majesties,
above the fruited plain!
America! America!
God shed his grace on thee,
And crown thy good with brotherhood,
From sea to shining sea.

America (My Country 'Tis of Thee)

My country 'tis of thee,
Sweet land of liberty,
Of thee I sing;
Land where my fathers died,
Land of the Pilgrim's pride,
From every mountainside,
Let freedom ring.

The Star-Spangled Banner (The National Anthem)

Oh, say, can you see,
by the dawn's early light,
What so proudly we hailed
at the twilight's last gleaming?
Whose broad stripes and bright stars,
through the perilous fight,
O'er the ramparts we watched,
were so gallantly streaming?
And the rockets' red glare,
the bombs bursting in air,
Gave proof through the night
that our flag was still there.
Oh, say, does that star-spangled
banner yet wave
O'er the land of the free
and the home of the brave?

Yankee Doodle

Yankee Doodle dates from pre-Revolutionary times in America. A *yankee* is a person living in the British colony. *Doodle* is a name. *Macaroni* was a fancy Italian clothing style that was popular in England at the time. There are numerous verses to the song.

Yankee Doodle went to town
A-riding on a pony
Stuck a feather in his hat
And called it macaroni.

Yankee Doodle, keep it up
Yankee Doodle dandy
Mind the music and the step
And with the girls be handy.

Father and I went down to camp
Along with Captain Gooding
And there we saw the men and boys
As thick as hasty pudding.

Yankee Doodle, keep it up
Yankee Doodle dandy
Mind the music and the step
And with the girls be handy.

Pledge of Allegiance

I pledge allegiance to the flag
of the United States of America,
and to the republic for which it stands,
one nation, under God, indivisible,
with liberty and justice for all.

Oath of Allegiance

I hereby declare, on oath, that I absolutely and entirely renounce and abjure all allegiance and fidelity to any foreign prince, potentate, state or sovereignty, of whom or which I have heretofore been a subject or a citizen; that I will support and defend the Constitution and laws of the United States of America against all enemies, foreign and domestic; that I will bear true faith and allegiance to the same; that I will bear arms on behalf of the United States when required by the law; that I will perform noncombatant service in the armed forces of the United States when required by the law; that I will perform work of national importance under civilian direction when required by the law; and that I take this obligation freely without any mental reservation or purpose of evasion; so help me God.

Index

Credits